MW01169441

ANNIVERSARY CLOCK IDENTIFICATION

by

Mervyn Passmore

Copyright notice
First published 2009

© Mervyn Passmore 2009, 2013

First edition   2009
Second edition   April 2013

Acknowledgements
The Horolovar Company, Box 942 Lancaster, Ohio OH 43130 USA. Publishers of 'The Horolovar 400 Day Repair Guide'
Horolovar is a registered Trademark of the Horolovar Company

Published by
Mervyn W. Passmore
London England

All clocks shown in this publication are in the Passmore Collection, a private collection of Anniversary Clocks.

Second Edition
2.0a

In memory of the late Charles Terwilliger, author of the Horolovar 400 Day Clock Repair Guide, and the late Karl Kochmann, author of The Clock & Watch Trade Marks Index, The Gustav Becker Story and other reference books on German clockmaking, both of whom encouraged me to take an interest in these clocks many years ago.

Without their support and advice in the 1980's, my knowledge of Anniversary Clocks and German clockmaking would be a fraction of what it is today.

The Passmore Collection is a private collection of Anniversary Clocks.

All the photographs used in this book were taken using clocks from

Unfortunately the collection is not on public display and is currently in storage.

Introduction

Anniversary Clocks were first produced commercially in the late 1800's by a number of German clock factories, but it was not until the early 1900's that mass production of any volume began. Since then, millions have been manufactured in a wide variety of styles and sizes, by a fairly small number of factories, mostly in Germany.

A mechanical clock that will run for a year or more between windings is a delicate piece of engineering. It depends on being placed on a solid surface, in a draught free environment, and above all, being serviced regularly to prevent friction building up within the train of gears.

The design concept of most of these clocks is the rotating or torsion pendulum, which hangs on a delicate spring steel suspension. If this suspension wire becomes distorted or interfered with, the clock will have difficulty running, and will probably not go for the full duration it was designed to run for.

Those involved in the sale, valuation or repair of these clocks need to be able to identify the models concerned, whether it be to obtain spare suspension wires or other parts, or simply to be able to describe it accurately. The purpose of this book is to enable anyone, professional or amateur, to identify the movement used in a clock quickly and accurately, and to be able to obtain information about the model, the manufacturer and the parts is uses.

How to use this book

The whole intention of this book is to create a source of information that will enable the reader to identify a clock quickly. The book can be read from start to finish by anyone wanting to learn about the manufacturers and models, but to identify a clock quickly it is important to use the tools provided.

If you *know* the name of the manufacturer, and here we mean the true name, not a retailer's name that might be on the dial or a misleading importer's name on the backplate, then turn to the list of manufacturers on page 25

If there is a logo or some text that you think might lead you to discover the name of the manufacturer, turn to the list of logos on page 27 or the groups of movements on page 21.

Failing that, or in case of any doubt, turn to the list of backplate dimensions on page 31. To use that list, all you need to measure is the width and height of the backplate and the gap between the plates.

If someone gives you a **Movement Identity Code**, turn to the **MIC** code listings on page 29, and look up the page number.

The principal manufacturers

These firms were the principal manufacturers of Anniversary Clock movements and clocks. It is common to find movements stamped with the importer's name or trademark, but these firms were not manufacturers. For example, Henry Coehler Co. Inc of New York (HECO) can frequently be found on German movements. In the UK, BHA (B. H. Abrahams) can often be found on Gustav Becker clocks. Neither firm manufactured 400 day clocks.

Company name	Trademark or logo
Andreas Huber****	Huber Uhren
Badische Uhrenfabrik****	B
Edgar Henn	EHF
Franz Hermle & Söhne	FHS
Franz Vosseler	Fr Vosseler
Gebrüder Junghans Uhrenfabrik	Junghans
Georg Würthner	Wurthner Western
Gerson Wintermantel	R
Grivolas**	Pendules 400 jours
Gustav Becker	GB
Hettich	Hettich
Jahresuhrenfabrik August Schatz & Söhne****	Jahresuhrenfabrik & Schatz
Kaiser	Kaiser
Kern & Link (later to become Kerne & Söhne)	
Kern & Söhne	KS
Kieninger & Obergfell	Kundo
Kienzle Clock Factories (later to become Kern & Link)	
Konrad Mauch	Koma
Link	
Neueck	
Nisshin Clock Industrial Co. Ltd**	Master
Philip Hauck***	
Schlenker & Posner	
Schneckenburger	RSM
Siegfried Haller	Haller
Staiger	
Uhrenfabrik Herr*	
Uhrenfabrik Neueck*	Neueck
Uhrenfabrik Reiner*	
W. A. Shmid-Schlenker Jr. GmbH & Co.	
W. Petersen	(Kaiser)
Wintermantel GmbH	W
W Würth & Co	

*Uhrenfabrik Herr and Uhrenfabrik Reiner worked very closely together and in many respects the parts appear to have come from same tooling. Their listings have been combined in this book. Neueck took over the two companies when they went bankrupt.

** All the firms in this list were based in Germany with the exception of the Nisshin Clock Industrial Co. Ltd. of Japan and Grivolas of France.

***It appears that the Horolovar 400 day Clock Repair Guide erroneously attributed Hauck's clocks to Philip Haas & Co. as there is evidence to suggest that Philip Haas never manufactured a single Anniversary clock.

These importers names are frequently found on backplates, but they were not manufacturers of anniversary clocks

Name on plate	Real name	Sources of movements
Becken	A C Becken & Co	Kern, Kieninger & Obergfell
BHA	B. H. Abrahams Ltd.	Gustav Becker
Coehler & Co	H. Coehler & Co	Almost every mass producer
Cuckoo Clock. Co	Cuckoo Clock Mfg Co	Herr/Reiner, Henn, K&O
Euramca	Euramca Trading Corp	Henn, Herr/Reiner, K & O
Forrestville	Forestville Clock Co. Inc	Henn, Herr/Reiner
Hall Craft	Hall Craft Corp	Herr/Reiner
Hudson	The J. L. Hudson Co.	Kieninger & Obergfell
John Wanamaker		Herr/Reiner
Urania	Urania GmbH (an exporter)	Hauck, Kienzle, Gustav Becker
Welby	Welby Corp.	Kieninger & Obergfell

Some typical importer's names and logos

Identification methods

Alphabetical listings
Movements are listed in the identification section in alphabetical order of manufacturer, but this is not the most efficient way to identify a clock, partly because many plates have no name or logo on them, and some bear misleading importer's names or logos. The alphabetical listings are for final verification of the exact model, and for further information.

Plate sizes
By far the quickest way to identify a clock is by combination of any name or logo and the plate sizes. Simply identify the correct plate size from the table and consult every listing of that size until you find the correct movement.

Obvious characteristics
An expert will be able to recognize many small and simple characteristics immediately, and this knowledge can be of great help, particularly when making online auction purchases. The shape of a click to the style of a locking device can be all it takes to identify a movement. Many tips are shown on the identification pages as **Rapid Recognition Tips.**

Warnings
Never assume that two identical cases will have the same movement inside.

Never put too much faith in a pendulum, dial or other item that may have been married up or replaced in the past.

Some of the early standard movements look extraordinarily similar to the inexperienced eye, and there are a few models that experts cannot fully agree on.

Plate measurements are given to the nearest millimetre. Whilst later movements were mass produced and therefore consistent, early plates were hand finished. The height and width of early examples of the same movement can vary by a millimetre or so.

If you cannot identify your clock
Check www.AnniversaryClockIdentification.com for any updated information, or post a request on the website at www.anniversaryclocks.org.

Contact the publisher with a clear photo of the back plate of the clock and its dimensions.

Mistakes can be made in factories.

Here is an example of a Schatz 49 incorrectly stamped in the factory as a Schatz 54. A Schatz 54 exists in two shapes; one with straight legs and one with curved legs. A Schatz 54 is a 1,000 day clock, totally different to a Schatz 49.

It is important not to jump to conclusions or to depend too heavily on one fact alone.

Clearly stamped '54'

The clock has a rectangular back plate and is identical to a Schatz 49

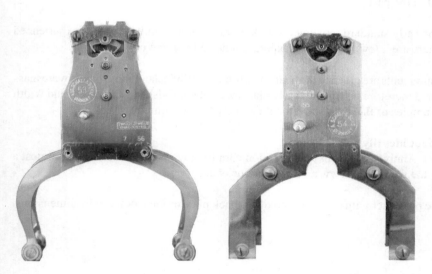

The Schatz 54s are totally different to the Schatz 49.

Movement sizes and names

Movements in this book have been classified by generic names, rather than by manufacturers' names. During the first 70 years of the 20th century, the movements in these clocks changed in size several times, resulting in four generic movement types.

Standard
This was the size of plate that most movements were made to until around 1950. Most were in the region of 70mm wide and 90mm high.

Standard Narrow
From the early 1950's manufacturers realised that by reducing the plate width to around 45mm (1.77"), the clocks could enter the USA as a watch as opposed to a clock, thereby attracting a lower rate of import duty due to outdated customs classifications. Most models use exactly the same gears in the standard and standard narrow versions.

Edgar Henn and others cunningly produced narrow movements with detachable plate extensions. Henn's movement was imported by the Euramca Trading Corporation at the watch tariff. Prior to sale, the plate extensions were fitted, giving the appearance of a standard and therefore more up-market movement.

Miniature
The next development was the miniature movement, a substantially smaller and more advanced clock. The width generally remained similar to the standard narrow movement, but the height dropped to around 60mm.

Henn's movement with side extensions fitted.

Midget
Finally, the fourth group of movements emerged, to cater for the demand for much more compact clocks under smaller domes. The width remained similar but the height dropped to around 55mm.

Confusingly, Kieninger & Obergfell modified their miniature movement and turned it into a midget without reducing the plate size. They cut out a large rectangle from the bottom of the backplate of the miniature movement, so that the pendulum could be raised significantly. The cut-out allowed the pendulum hook to be above the platform without fouling the plates. A squat pendulum and a different suspension turned it into a Midget.

Miniature   *Midget*

Not everyone kept to these generic names, and it is common to see references to models such as Junior and Baby.

To avoid confusion, all the movements in this book are classified using the generic family names wherever appropriate.

The Kundo range is a good example of the evolution of the models.

The Kundo with a Standard movement

The Kundo with a Standard Narrow movement. Apart from a more modern style, the clock was of the same appearance as those with the wider movement.

The Kundo with a Miniature movement was shorter than the Standard models but kept to the original shape.

The Kundo with a Miniature movement was fitted with a re-designed bob that reduced the height without modification to the movement.

The Kundo Miniature movement in what was the smallest style of its kind ever produced.

The Kundo Midget movement evolved and suited smaller homes and smaller mantelpieces but kept to traditional proportions.

On each identification page a list of data is provided:

Plate shape
Rectangular, Round, Legged, Vest shape or Triangular

Plate width
Width of the backplate in millimetres, to the nearest millimetre.

Plate height
Height of the backplate in millimetres, to the nearest millimetre.

Gap between plates
This is the internal gap between the plates in millimetres, to the nearest millimetre.

Escapement type
Dead beat or Pin Pallet. Please refer to the descriptions overleaf.

Original key size
The distance between the flat surfaces of the nearest standard key when the clock was new.

Winding side
Left or Right when viewed from the winding shaft.

Pivot adjuster - Please refer to the descriptions overleaf.
Eccentric nut. A round bush in the plate with a slot to enable it to be rotated with a screwdriver
Screwed bracket. Normally combined with the suspension support
Adjustable arm. The pivot hole is in an arm cut out of the backplate that can be bent if necessary.

Locking device
Position and style of the locking system.

Pendulum type/s
Known types, such as Disc, 3-ball, 4-ball etc.

Mainspring barrel
Width and diameter of the spring barrel in millimetres

Replacement wire
Standard wire number, followed by the Horolovar™ size

Replacement unit
The appropriate complete suspension unit code and the Horolovar number

Jig settings
The distance between the top of the bottom block and the fork followed by the distance between the top of the bottom block and the bottom of the top block.

Mainspring
The width, strength and diameter of the nearest suitable spring, followed by the length in brackets. e.g. 13 x 0.35 x 30mm (970mm)

Beats per minute
The number of rotations of the pendulum per minute. This is the total number of escapement ticks per minute, not complete turns of the bob.

Bob weight
The typical weight of a pendulum, but others can exist.

Movement Identity Code (MIC)
Each movement has been given a unique identity code (MIC), to avoid confusion when readers refer to a particular movement. This is particularly useful when a manufacturer made changes to a movement during production; for example in the case of Konrad Mauch who changed the size of the mainsprings on two movements.

Escapement types

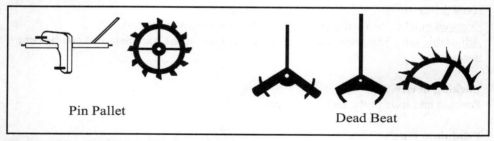

Pin Pallet　　　　　　　　　　　　　　　　Dead Beat

Pivot adjustment methods

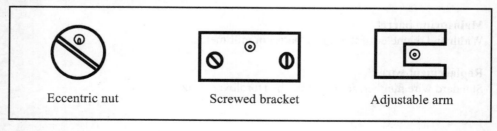

Eccentric nut　　　　　　Screwed bracket　　　　　Adjustable arm

Recognition by pendulum bob

It is not normally a good idea to try to identify a clock from something so interchangeable as a pendulum bob. Many have become detached from their clocks over the years, and subsequently married up with another clock. However sometimes it is useful to have some re-assurance that the bob is correct. Many early clocks can be very hard to identify and it can be the small clues like the bob, the guard etc that help make the final decision.

The huge permutation of the shapes of the balls and their arms can be confusing and so it pays use simple clues whenever possible. One such clue is the style of the inscription on the adjuster. Pendulum shapes changed frequently but many manufacturers kept the same style of text and arrows.

Typical Kieninger & Obergfell

The simple A|R on the early models. Later it became just + -

The unmistakable Kundo 'hook' with its washers and coiled spring on post war models.

Jahresuhrenfabrik Aug. Schatz & Söhne

Siegfried Haller

The graduated time track and arrows remained the same for many years, as did the two holes that later formed part of the locking mechanism.

Typical Haller inscription before they introduced plain ones, because the inscription was on the bracket on later clocks.

The Haller plastic hook

The Gustav Becker bob with screwed gallery.

Often the Becker bob has the number written underneath in ink.

The Gustav Becker Ball pendulum.

The Kern ceramic dancers.

The Hauck pendulum often had a very narrow gallery, without screws.

The badische 3-ball pendulum. Actually it has 5, including the two central balls.

The Kaiser hollow Globe.

The Kundo Square Ball.

The stylish Grivolas bob with its weights concealed inside.

The 'Snakes & Balls' often seen on Würth clocks.

The Junghans 2-ball.

One of Jahresuhrenfabrik's earliest.

Rapid Recognition by style

Many makers maintained a consistent style or feature that provides an immediate clue when identifying.

The Kundo locking device, used on all later torsion movements, is an immediate way to identify the manufacturer.

Distinctive Badische pediment

One of several Jahresuhrenfabrik A. Schatz legged plates.

A typical Kaiser globe

The distinctive Koma cut-out in most back plates.

Kienzle's distinctive double pairs of guard holes on back plates.

P. Hauck's top block support.

Gustav Becker's guard supports.

18

Things you are likely to see

The range and variety of these clocks makes it impossible to show every style and design for every manufacturer. Here are some less common features you may come across.

Clocks in wooden cases

Gimbal top block supports

The cap fitted to tubular suspension guards

The Gustav Becker complex beat adjuster.

Typical double ended key for disc pendulums.

Gilded Deco cases

Bandstand cases

During the transition between disc to ball pendulums, extensions were sometimes fitted.

Identification isn't always a simple answer

Here we have an example of how difficult it can be to identify a clock fully, and that one must not jump to conclusions. The clock in question is a standard model, chrome plated. In the bottom right-hand corner we have the Badische logo, namely the letter B in a crescent moon. It hasn't been scratched on by someone; it was clearly done prior to plating. However, there is nothing 'Badische' about the backplate. In fact, it matches the criteria of a Jahresuhrenfabrik Standard movement in every way. Even the clock has the same pillars, the same

pendulum, the same finials and the same pediment as a Jahresuhrenfabrik clock.

Both clock movements are 66mm x 88mm and the gaps are 30mm. Looking at the photos below, you can see that the plates are identical and the fittings are identical but that the chrome backplate on the left is clearly marked with the Badische logo and the brass plate on the right has the Jahresuhrenfabrik Elephant logo.

It is important to decide the purpose of the identification. Obviously one would classify the clock as a Badische, but if you need to select a suspension, you have to accept that the movement of this clock was made by Jahresuhrenfabrik A. Schatz & Söhne. In fact Badische bought movements from Jahresuhrenfabrik and vast numbers of lantern pinion movements from Andreas Huber. Huber worked closely with Kienzle Clock Factories, so it is common to find a clock with Kienzle on the dial that appears to have a Badische movement in it.

In the same way, J. Kaiser stamped the Kaiser name and address on the back of movements clearly made by W. Petersen.

The Badische example

The Jahresuhrenfabrik example

The Badische Uhrenfabrik and Jahresuhrenfabrik clocks that must share the same origins.

The Badische Uhrenfabrik example   *The Jahresuhrenfabrik example*

The ease of identification of an Anniversary Clock generally falls into one of four distinct groups:

- Very easy to identify
- Fairly easy to identify
- Not immediately identifiable
- Hard to identify

The very easy ones are shown below. If your clock bears one of these inscriptions, you can turn directly to the page shown and verify the information:

K.u.S. PI 13-31
K.u.S. MIV 13-23
K.u.S. SIV 13-11
Aug. Schatz 49 11-11
Aug. Schatz JUM/7 11-15
Grivolas 8-3
Gustav Becker or GB in an anchor 9-3

The fairly easy ones can normally be identified very quickly, but there may be a choice of models or a change during manufacture meaning that you will need to choose from one or more possible alternatives. The logos are illustrated on page 27.

The Elephant logo 11-1
The Badische B 1-1
The KOMA logo 16-1
Aug. Schatz 53 .... 11-19, 11-23
Aug. Schatz 54 .... 11-27, 11-31
The KS logo 13-1
Kundo trademark 14-1
The somewhat confusing KO logo 14-1
Schnekenburger 22-1

Those not immediately identifiable include clock plates with importers' names disguising the true manufacturer, and those that despite being mass produced were sold without any inscription except perhaps 'Germany' or West Germany'. If the name on the plate is not listed in the list of principal firms earlier, then use the plate dimension tables. Remember that West Germany implies postwar, helping with dating a clock.

Many factories stamped the importers' names on their movements. Some importers purchased from more than one factory. Some of the logos are shown on page 8.

Importers' marks

Mark	Importer	Purchased from
Becken	A C Becken & Co.	Kern, Kieninger & Obergfell
BHA	B. H. Abrahams	Gustav Becker
Coehler & Co.	H. Coehler & Co.	Almost every mass producer
Cuckoo Clock Co.	Cuckoo Clock Mfg. Co.	Herr/Reiner, Henn, K&O
Euramca	Euramca Trading Corp.	Henn, Herr/Reiner, K & O
Forrestville	Forestville Clock Co. Inc.	Henn, Herr/Reiner
Hall Craft	Hall Craft Corp.	Herr/Reiner
J L Hudson Co.		Kieninger & Obergfell
John Wanamaker		Herr/Reiner
Urania	Urania GmbH	Hauck, Kienzle, Gustav Becker
Welby	Welby Corp.	Kieninger & Obergfell

The **final group of hard to identify clocks** mainly comprises of unmarked clocks with plates of around 66mm wide and 88mm high. This was a common size from the turn of the century. If you need to identify one of these, you may need to use the plate dimension tables to identify each possibility and then study the images of the backplates carefully. When the Jahresuhrenfabrik patent expired on their standard clock, it was copied by several firms. Some are more distinctive than others, but the majority have a characteristic that makes them identifiable.

The 43mm x 70mm group of unmarked plates

Only one manufacturer sold plates of this size unmarked, but more than model exists. Refer to the list of models made by Uhrenfabrik Herr & Uhrenfabrik Reiner.

The 43mm x 75mm group of unmarked plates

Only one manufacturer sold plates of this size unmarked. Refer to the list of models made by Edgar Henn.

The 43mm x 94mm group of unmarked plates

Only two manufacturers sold plates of this size unmarked.

Edgar Henn made a movement 43mm x 94mm with a very distinctive replaceable eccentric nut.

Henn's replaceable eccentric nut.

Uhrenfabrik Herr & Reiner made a movement 43mm x 94mm with a _vertical ratchet support_, and round corners, held together with screws. Refer to the Uhrenfabrik Herr and Uhrenfabrik Reiner pages.

The 66mm x 88mm group of unmarked plates
The large group of movements sized 66mm x 88mm has the following main members. Sizes close to the 66mm x 88mm group have been included.

Kienzle made a 66mm x 87mm movement that was frequently unmarked except for a serial number. Many have a distinctive pair of "Double holes" on the back-plate, on a plate with an _internal_ ratchet.

The two pairs of distinctive holes, on a Kienzle plate with an internal ratchet.

Philip Hauck made a 66mm x 88mm movement that was unmarked except for a serial number, normally close to a _vertical_ ratchet wheel cut from solid brass. Complex suspension support.

The **Jahresuhrenfabrik Original** was 66mm x 88mm and was normally unmarked The plates were thicker than the Standard Early at about 2.4mm. Sometimes marked Patent Angemeldet or D.R.P. The _horizontal ratchet_ wheel support is normally made from solid brass.

Philip Hauck's distinctive support and vertical solid ratchet support.

The **Jahresuhrenfabrik Standard Early** was 66mm x 88mm and was often unmarked, or marked Made in Germany in an arc above the serial number. Sometimes stamped with a small letter in the very bottom left corner of the backplate. Very often you will see the guard screws as just undrilled dots on this early model.

The ratchet wheel support is made from one piece, like those by P. Hauck, but horizontal.

The **Jahresuhrenfabrik Standard 49** was 66mm x 88mm and was sometimes unmarked. Similar to the Standard Early model but with Inspection holes. The Standard 40 normally has a gap between the platform and the movement.

Typical gap between the platform and pinned plates with square corners.

Uhrenfabrik Herr & Reiner made a movement 66mm x 88mm that was sold unmarked. The plates have rounded corners, and the back-plate is screwed on, not pinned. There is a gap between the platform and the movement, like many Jahresuhrenfabrik clocks, but this backplate has rounded corners and screwed plates.

The 72mm x 93mm group of unmarked plates

Only one manufacturer sold plates of this size unmarked. Refer to the list of models used by Badische Uhrenfabrik.

Typical gap between the platform and screwed plates with rounded corners.

Alphabetical listings

The following pages contain information in alphabetical order of manufacturer. Each manufacturer is ordered in diminishing plate size, which also acts as a general chronological order. If you can identify the factory from this list, turn to the appropriate section where you will find a list of movements.

Manufacturer	Trademark	Section
Badische Uhrenfabrik	B	1
Edgar Henn	EHF	2
Franz Hermle & Söhne	FHS	3
Franz Vosseler	Fr Vosseler	4
Gebrüder Junghans Uhrenfabrik		5
George Würthner	Wurthner Western	6
Gerson Wintermantel	R	7
Grivolas	Pendules 400 jours	8
Gustav Becker	G B	9
Hettich		10
Jahresuhrenfabrik A. Schatz & Söhne	Schatz	11
J. Kaiser**	Kaiser	12
Kern & Söhne	KS	13
Kieninger & Obergfell	Kundo, KO	14
Kienzle		15
Konrad Mauch	Koma	16
Link		17
Master Nisshin Clock Industrial Co. Ltd**	Master	18
Neueck		19
P Hauck		20
Schlenker & Posner		21
Shnekenburger		22
Siegfried Haller	Haller	23
Staiger		24
Uhrenfabrik Herr*		25
Uhrenfabrik Reiner*		25
W. A. Shmid-Schlenker Jr. GmbH & Co.		26
W. Peterson	(Kaiser)	27
Wintermantel	W	28
Würth W.		29

* Uhrenfabrik Herr and Uhrenfabrik Reiner worked very closely together and in many respects the parts appear to have come from same tooling. Their listings have been combined in this book.
** Some Kaiser movements were bought from W. Petersen and stamped with the Kaiser marks.

The sections are in alphabetical order in terms of the full company names, but sometimes more the familiar nicknames are used, generally being the lastname with the firstname of initial dropped. Jahresuhrenfabrik Aug. Schatz & Söhne is shortened to JUF Schatz.

Temperature compensation

One of the biggest problems facing the early manufacturers was that these clocks would go slower in warm weather. Numerous different schemes were employed to correct this, but few of them worked. The best ones used bimetallic strips.

The problem was finally solved when the Horolovar Company manufactured wires out of special nickel alloys that changed negligibly when the ambient temperature changed. It was not the change in length that was causing the problem - it was the reduction in stiffness that occurred when the wire was warmer.

The large coil on the right of the pendulum above shortened the effective length of the suspension wire. The wire passes through a slot in the coil. When the temperature increases the coil opens. This makes the slot rise, thus shortening the wire in use. The coil on the left is decorative and acts as a counterbalance.

The disc above has been replaced with brass weights on bimetallic strips. As the temperature changes the diameter of the bob automatically adjusts.

The Jahresuhrenfabrik bob that appeared to be temperature compensating

Kienzle's version of the mercury Compensating bob. In fact it had little effect.

Wurth's 'Snakes & Balls' gave the appearance of compensation

Rapid Recognition by logo

Although few of the early clocks had logos or makers' names stamped on the plates, the majority of later clocks have marks that will identify the factory.

Badische
Uhrenfabrik

Franz Hermle

Georg Würthner

Grivolas of France

Herr

Gustav Becker

Jahresuhrenfabrik Aug. Schatz & Söhne.

Kerne &
Söhne

Kieninger & Obergfell

Konrad Mauch

J Link & Co

Nisshin

R M Schneckenberger

Siegfried Haller

W Petersen

Wintermantel

German-English translations of common words and abbreviations found on Anniversary Clocks:

D.R.G.M. .... Deutsche Reich Gebrauchs Muster (a Registered design)
D.R.P .... Deutsche Reiche Patent (a patent)
Gebrüder .... Brother
GmbH .... Gesellschaft mit beschränkter Haftung (Ltd Co.)
Jahr .... Year
Jahresuhr .... Year going clock
Söhne .... Son
Und .... And (as in K und O for Kundo)
Uhrenfabrik .... Clock factory

U.S.P .... United States Patent

Movement Identity Codes

Movement Identity Codes (MICs) are unique alphanumeric codes that refer to a particular movement. There may be slight variations between examples, such as the name of an importer in place of the manufacturer, or incidental differences such as unused holes etc. Using these codes you can refer to a particular movement when ordering parts, offering a clock for sale or taking part in an online discussion.

You can also use them on this book's website at www.AnniversaryClockIdentification.com to create a temporary online page for use when you want to describe a clock to someone who does not have a copy of this book.

Movement Identity Codes

AH-2S Badische Std doube semis 1-7
AH-30 Badische Std. 30 day 1-19
AH-SE Badische Standard Early 1-3
AH-SU Badische Std. U 1-11
AH-SV Badische Std. V 1-15
EH-MIN Henn Miniature 2-7
EH-SN Henn Standard narrow 2-3
FH-MIN Hermle Miniature 3-7
FH-STD Hermle Standard 3-3
FV-60 Vosseler small 60mm 4-3
GB-STD Becker Standard 9-3
GJ-90 Junghans Circular 90mm 5-3
GR-DE Grivolas German 8-7
GR-FR Grivolas French 8-3
GS-60 Staiger Round 24-3
GW-SN Würthner Western Std Narrow 6-3
HE-REM Hettich Remontoire 10-3
HR-MINE Herr/Reiner Miniature Early 25-11
HR-ML10 Herr/Reiner Mini Late 10" 25-15
HR-ML8 Herr/Reiner Mini Late 8" 25-19
HR-SNR Herr/Reiner Standard Narrow 25-7
HR-STD Herr/Reiner Standard 25-3
JK-SN Kaiser Standard narrow 12-3
JL-SN Link Standard Narrow 17-3
JS-53L Schatz Miniature 53 Legged 11-23
JS-53V Schatz Miniature 53 vest 11-19
JS-54C Schatz Mini 54 1,000 day Curved 11-31
JS-54S Schatz Min 54 1,000 day Straight 11-27
JS-59 Schatz Balance Wheel 59 11-43
JS-BA Schatz Miniature BA Rem. 11-35
JS-JUM7 Schatz Miniature 11-15
JS-S49 JUF Standard 49 11-11
JS-SE JUF Standard early 11-7

Identification by plate shape and size

Using this list, you can normally identify a clock movement very quickly. If more than one entry exists for the same size, be sure to check all the possible pages. For example, the Kieninger & Obergfell Miniature and Midget movements have plates of the same size but are quite different movements.

Legged
43mm x 60mm x 32mm Schatz Miniature 54 1,000 day 11-31
43mm x 66mm x 32mm Schatz Miniature 54 1,000 day 11-27
44mm x 66mm x 21mm Schatz Miniature 53 Legged 11-23
64mm x 101mm x 20mm Schatz Miniature 59 Bal. wheel 11-43

Rectangular
42mm x 54mm x 20mm Koma Midget Early 16-23
42mm x 54mm x 21mm Koma Midget late 16-27
42mm x 77mm x 25mm Koma miniature early 16-11
42mm x 77mm x 25mm Koma miniature late, ext. rat. 16-15
42mm x 77mm x 25mm Koma miniature late, int. rat. 16-19
42mm x 84mm x 31mm Haller Standard Narrow early 23-7
42mm x 84mm x 31mm Haller Standard Narrow Late 23-11
42mm x 93mm x 30mm Würthner Standard Narrow 6-3
43mm x 75mm x 30mm Henn Miniature 2-7
43mm x 94mm x 33mm Henn Standard extended narrow 2-3
44mm x 40mm x 19mm Hettich Remontoire 10-3
44mm x 54mm x 21mm Kern Midget KuS PI 13-31
44mm x 60mm x 20mm Kern Mini L/H wind, bracket 13-19
44mm x 60mm x 20mm Kern Mini L/H wind, eccentric 13-15
44mm x 60mm x 20mm Kern Miniature Remontoire 13-27
44mm x 60mm x 21mm Haller Midget early 23-23
44mm x 60mm x 21mm Haller Midget late 23-27
44mm x 60mm x 21mm Haller Miniature, early 23-15
44mm x 60mm x 21mm Haller Miniature, late 23-19
44mm x 60mm x 21mm Kern Mini MIV R/H winder 13-23
44mm x 70mm x 23mm Herr/Reiner Mini Late 10" 25-15
44mm x 70mm x 23mm Herr/Reiner Mini Late 8" 25-19
44mm x 70mm x 23mm Herr/Reiner Miniature Early 25-11
44mm x 70mm x 23mm K&O Midget 14-19
44mm x 70mm x 23mm K&O Miniature 14-15
44mm x 88mm x 30mm Kaiser Universe 12-3
44mm x 93mm x 30mm Herr/Reiner Standard Clockwise 25-7
44mm x 93mm x 30mm K&O Standard narrow 14-11
44mm x 93mm x 30mm Kern Standard narrow SIV 13-11
44mm x 93mm x 30mm Neueck Standard Narrow 19-3
44mm x 95mm x 31mmLink Standard Narrow 17-3
50mm x 91mm x 30mm Master Standard, round corners 18-3
55mm x 75mm x 24mm, Badische 30 day 1-19

Anniversary Clock Identification Chart

Start Here

by Mervyn Passmore

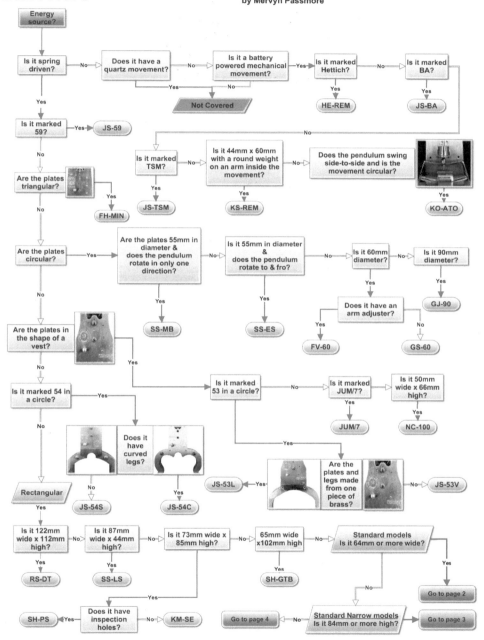

Energy source?

Is it spring driven? —No→ Does it have a quartz movement? —No→ Is it a battery powered mechanical movement? —Yes→ Is it marked Hettich? —No→ Is it marked BA?

Does it have a quartz movement? —Yes→

Is it a battery powered mechanical movement? —No→ Not Covered

Is it marked Hettich? Yes→ HE-REM

Is it marked BA? Yes→ JS-BA

Is it spring driven? Yes

Is it marked 59? —Yes→ JS-59

No

Are the plates triangular? —No→ Is it marked TSM? —No→ Is it 44mm x 60mm with a round weight on an arm inside the movement? —No→ Does the pendulum swing side-to-side and is the movement circular?

Are the plates triangular? Yes→ FH-MIN

Is it marked TSM? Yes→ JS-TSM

Is it 44mm x 60mm with a round weight on an arm inside the movement? Yes→ KS-REM

Does the pendulum swing side-to-side and is the movement circular? Yes→ KO-ATO

Are the plates circular? —Yes→ Are the plates 55mm in diameter & does the pendulum rotate in only one direction? —No→ Is it 55mm in diameter & does the pendulum rotate to & fro? —No→ Is it 60mm diameter? —No→ Is it 90mm diameter?

Are the plates 55mm in diameter & does the pendulum rotate in only one direction? Yes→ SS-MB

Is it 55mm in diameter & does the pendulum rotate to & fro? Yes→ SS-ES

Is it 60mm diameter? Yes→ Does it have an arm adjuster? Yes→ FV-60 / No→ GS-60

Is it 90mm diameter? Yes→ GJ-90

Are the plates in the shape of a vest? —No→ Is it marked 54 in a circle? —Yes→ ... Is it marked 53 in a circle? —No→ Is it marked JUM/7? —Yes→ JUM/7

Is it marked 53 in a circle? Is it 50mm wide x 66mm high? Yes→ NC-100

Are the plates in the shape of a vest? Yes→

Does it have curved legs? No→ JS-54S / Yes→ JS-54C

JS-53L ←Yes— Are the plates and legs made from one piece of brass? —No→ JS-53V

Is it marked 54 in a circle? No

Rectangular

Is it 122mm wide x 112mm high? —No→ Is it 87mm wide x 44mm high? —No→ Is it 73mm wide x 85mm high? —No→ 65mm wide x102mm high —No→ Standard models Is it 64mm or more wide?

Is it 122mm wide x 112mm high? Yes→ RS-DT

Is it 87mm wide x 44mm high? Yes→ SS-LS

65mm wide x102mm high Yes→ SH-GTB

Standard models Is it 64mm or more wide? Yes→ Go to page 2 / No→

SH-PS ←Yes— Does it have inspection holes? —No→ KM-SE

Go to page 4 —No→ Standard Narrow models Is it 84mm or more high? —Yes→ Go to page 3

Anniversary Clock Identification Chart 2
by Mervyn Passmore

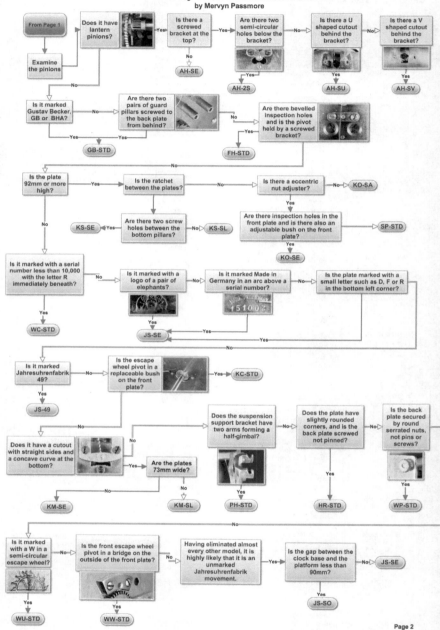

Anniversary Clock Identification Chart 3
by Mervyn Passmore

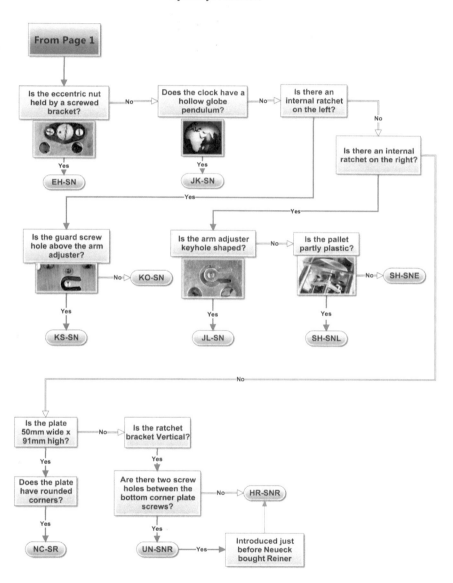

From Page 1

Is the eccentric nut held by a screwed bracket? —No→ Does the clock have a hollow globe pendulum? —No→ Is there an internal ratchet on the left?

No↓

Is there an internal ratchet on the right?

Yes↓ EH-SN

Yes↓ JK-SN

—Yes→

—Yes→

Is the guard screw hole above the arm adjuster?

Is the arm adjuster keyhole shaped? —No→ Is the pallet partly plastic?

—No→ KO-SN

—No→ SH-SNE

Yes↓ KS-SN

Yes↓ JL-SN

Yes↓ SH-SNL

—No—

Is the plate 50mm wide x 91mm high? —No→ Is the ratchet bracket Vertical?

Yes↓

Yes↓

Does the plate have rounded corners?

Are there two screw holes between the bottom corner plate screws? —No→ HR-SNR

Yes↓

Yes↓

NC-SR

UN-SNR —Yes→ Introduced just before Neueck bought Reiner

Anniversary Clock Identification Chart 4
by Mervyn Passmore

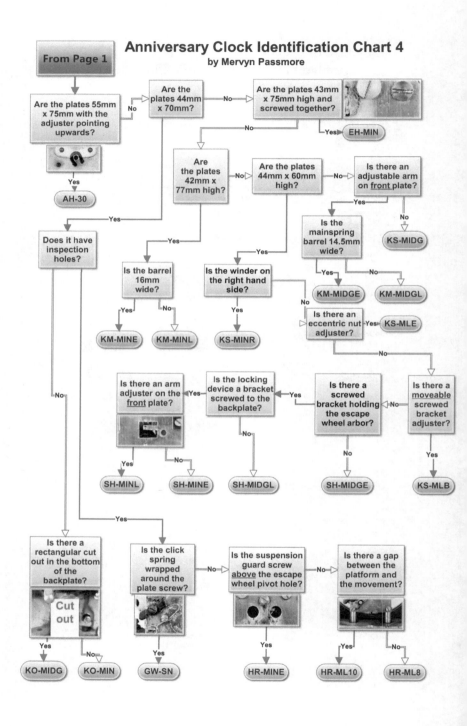

Badische Uhrenfabrik

Badische Uhrenfabrik has been described in the past as the manufacturer of the clocks in this section, and for the sake of convenience to users of this book, they remain so here. However, it seems likely that they bought them from Andreas Huber. In fact, many firms sold movements to each other in this way.

About 30% of "Badishe Uhrenfabrik" clocks bear the distinctive logo of a B within a crescent moon. It can be on the backplate, the dial and sometimes on the front plate beneath the dial. They sometimes purchased movements from Jahresuhrenfabrik A. Schatz. If it does not have lantern pinions, it is probably one of theirs.

The Badische Uhrenfabrik logo

This created, and still creates, much confusion over who made what.

Apart from the budget 30 day version, four common models exist, and three of these can be easily identified by the shape of the cut out at the top of the back plate. The plates are all a similar size.

Double semi-circles cutout.

Straight-sided cutout with a U curve at the bottom.

V-sided cutout with a squared bottom.

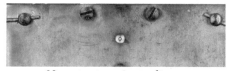

No cutout or pivot adjuster.

The Kienzle Clock Factories logo can appear on the dial, but Badische (Huber) movements were used widely in their 400 day clocks.

Badische Uhrenfabrik listings:

By model:

When a Badische Uhrenfabrik movement is used in a Kienzle clock, the platform normally has a large rectangular hole in it.

The distinctive Badische pediment often used.

Manufacturer:
Badische Uhrenfabrik

Model:
Badische Standard Early, 72mm x 91mm x 31mm

Backplate information:
Unmarked

Typical bracket on the early movement.

Movement ID code: **AH-SE**

Notes:
This movement was used widely on clocks made by Kienzle Clock Factories. It has no pivot adjuster. Although previously thought to have been manufactured by Badische, it is highly unlikely that Kienzle Clock Factories would have bought movements from them.

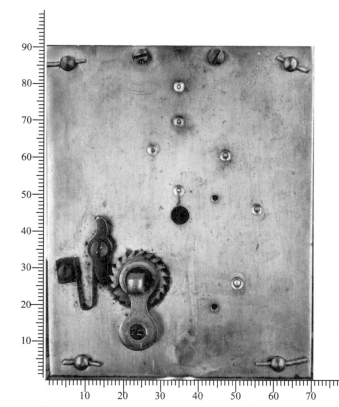

Badische Standard, Early
72 x 91 x 31mm

Notes
Despite Kienzle Clock Factories being a manufacturer, this Badische/Huber movement was used widely in their 400 day clocks.

Due to variations in suspension supports and bobs, you may have to use blocks and wires other than those shown.

Lantern pinions are made with wires, not solid steel.

No pivot adjuster.

Rapid Recognition Tips
Very few 400 day clocks have lantern pinions. These, combined with a 72mm x 91mm plate with no pivot adjuster, indicate this movement.

Data
Movement ID Code	**AH-SE**
Plate shape	**Rectangular**
Plate width	**72mm**
Plate height	**91mm**
Gap between plates	**31mm**
Escapement type	**Pin pallet**
Original key size	**4.50mm**
Winding side	**Left**
Pivot adjuster	**None**
Locking device:	**None**
Pendulum type/s	**4-ball**
Mainspring barrel	**22.5mm x 43mm**
Replacement wire	**No. 17 (Horolovar™ 0.0037"/0.094mm)**
Replacement unit	**None, you must assemble your own**
Jig settings	**118mm, 130mm**
Mainspring	**20 x 0.40 x 38mm (1350mm)**
Beats per minute	**8**
Bob weight	**280g.**

Examples of clocks fitted with the Badische Uhrenfabrik/Huber early movement

 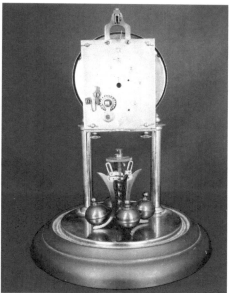

Manufacturer:

Badische Uhrenfabrik

Backplate information:

**B inside a crescent moon
Made in Germany**

Model:

**Badische Standard,
double semicircles
72mm x 93mm x 31mm**

Movement ID code: **AH-2S**

Notes:

This movement is distinctive by the double semicircles which act as inspection holes. Not to be confused with the normally unbranded movements with single 'U' or V cut.

Note the double semi-circles

*The distinctive
Badische 3-ball
pendulum.*

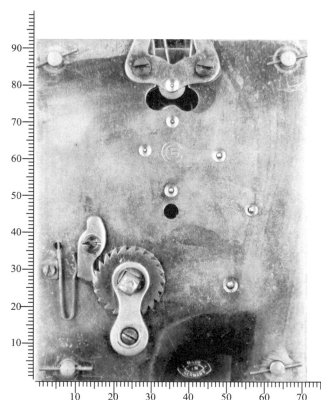

Badische Standard, double semi-circles
72 x 93 x 31mm

Notes

Lantern pinions.

Two similar but unmarked movements can be found. The other two do not have the double semi-circles. All four standard movements normally have a distinctive unused hole in the centre of the plate.

There does not seem to be a suitable wire available for some pendulums and it may be necessary to thin a standard suspension wire slightly. *Due to variations, you may have to use blocks and wires other than those shown.*

Lantern pinions are made with wires and not solid cut teeth.

Rapid Recognition Tips

These double semi-circles are unique to this movement.

Very few 400 day clocks have lantern pinions.

Note the double semi-circles

Data

Movement ID Code **AH-2S**
Plate shape .... **Rectangular**
Plate width **72mm**
Plate height **93mm**
Gap between plates **31mm**
Escapement type .... **Dead beat**
Original key size .... **4.25mm & 1.75mm**
Winding side .... **Left**
Pivot adjuster.............. **Screwed bracket**
Locking device: .... **None**
Pendulum type/s .... **Disc, 3-ball**
Mainspring barrel .... **22.5mm x 44mm**
Replacement wire .... **No. 15 (Horolovar™ 0.0035"/0.089mm)**
Replacement unit .... **None, you must assemble your own**
Jig settings .... **103mm, 115 or 118, 130mm**
Mainspring .... **20 x 0.40 x 38mm (1350mm)**
Beats per minute **8**
Bob weight .... **355g.**

Examples of clocks fitted with the Badische Uhrenfabrik/Huber double semi-circle movement

Manufacturer:
Badische Uhrenfabrik

Backplate information:

Unmarked

Model:
Badische Standard
'U' shape cut out
72mm x 93mm x 31mm

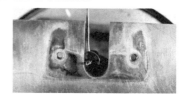

Note the straight-sided cutout with a curve at the bottom.

Movement ID code: **AH-SU**

Notes:
This movement is distinctive by being similar to the double semi-circle movement, but has only a single 'U' at the base of the cutout. This is normally hidden by the top bracket.

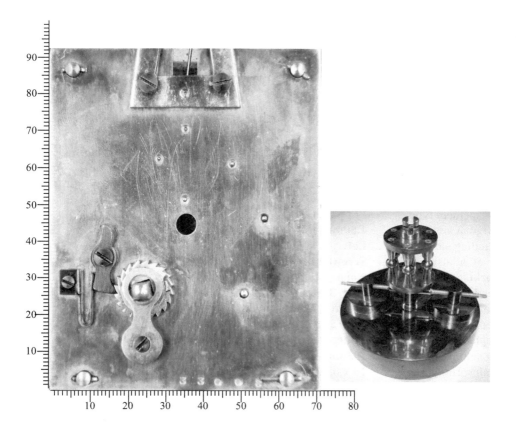

**Badische Standard, 'U' shape cut out
72 x 93 x 31mm**

Notes

A similarly unmarked Badische movement can be found with a square V cutout. All four Badische Standard movements normally have a distinctive unused hole in the centre of the plate, probably for assembly purposes.

Lantern pinions.

Lantern pinions are made with wires and not solid cut teeth.

Due to variations in bobs, you may have to use blocks and wires other than those shown. The 3-ball bob uses a shorter wire and a smaller bottom block.

Rapid Recognition Tips

This 'U' shape cutout is unique to this movement. Look for it from the inside because it is normally hidden by the bracket.

Very few 400 day clocks have lantern pinions.

Note the straight-sided cutout with a curve at the bottom.

Data

Movement ID Code	**AH-SU**
Plate shape	**Rectangular**
Plate width	**72mm**
Plate height	**93mm**
Gap between plates	**31mm**
Escapement type	**Pin pallet**
Original key size	**4.50mm**
Winding side	**Left**
Pivot adjuster	**Screwed bracket**
Locking device:	**None**
Pendulum type/s	**Disc, 3-ball**
Mainspring barrel	**22mm x 42mm**
Replacement wire	**No. 15 (Horolovar™ 0.0035"/0.089mm)**
Replacement unit	**None, you must assemble your own**
Jig settings	**103mm, 115mm or 118mm, 130mm**
Mainspring	**20 x 0.40 x 38mm (1350mm)**
Beats per minute	**8**
Bob weight	**395g.**

Examples of clocks fitted with the Badische Uhrenfabrik/Huber 'U' shape cutout movement

Manufacturer:
Badische Uhrenfabrik

Backplate information:
Unmarked

Model:
Badische Standard
Square V cut-out
72mm x 93mm x 31mm

Note the V-sided cutout with a squared bottom.

Movement ID code: **AH-SV**

Notes:

This movement is distinctive by being similar the to the unbranded 'U' shaped cut-out movement, but this one has a squared V cutout. This is normally hidden by the top bracket.

Badische Standard, square V cut-out
72 x 93 x 31mm

Notes
Lantern pinions.

A similarly unmarked Badische movement
can be found, with a 'U' shaped cut-out. All
four Standard movements used in Badische
clocks normally have a distinctive unused
hole in the centre of the plate, probably for
assembly purposes.
*Due to variations in bobs, you may have to
use blocks and wires other than those shown.
The 3-ball bob uses a shorter wire and a
smaller bottom block.*

*Most simple suspension
supports use a pin through
a hole in the support to
retain the top block. This
one uses a fixed top pin,
which sits in a slot in the
top.*

Rapid Recognition Tips
The distinctive 'V' cut in the backplate is unique
to this movement. Look for it from the inside of
the plate because it will be covered by the
bracket on the outside.
Very few 400 day clocks have lantern pinions.

Data
Movement ID Code ...... **AH-SV**
Plate shape .... **Rectangular**
Plate width **72mm**
Plate height **93mm**
Gap between plates **31mm**
Escapement type .... **Dead beat**
Original key size **4.50mm**
Winding side .... **Left**
Pivot adjuster .... **Screwed bracket**
Locking device: .... **None**
Pendulum type/s .... **Disc, 3-ball**
Mainspring barrel .... **22mm x 42mm**
Replacement wire .... **No. 15 (Horolovar™ 0.0035"/0.089mm)**
Replacement unit .... **None, you must assemble your own**
Jig settings .... **103mm, 115 or 118, 130mm**
Mainspring .... **20 x 0.40 x 38mm (1350mm)**
Beats per minute **8**
Bob weight .... **395g.**

Examples of clocks fitted with the Badische Uhrenfabrik/Huber V cut movement

Manufacturer:
Badische Uhrenfabrik

Model:
Badische Standard
30 Day
55mm x 75mm x 24mm

Backplate information:
Unmarked

Movement ID code: **AH-30**

Notes:
This Lunar movement runs for 30 days on its short, open loop mainspring.

Lantern pinions are made with wires and not solid cut teeth.

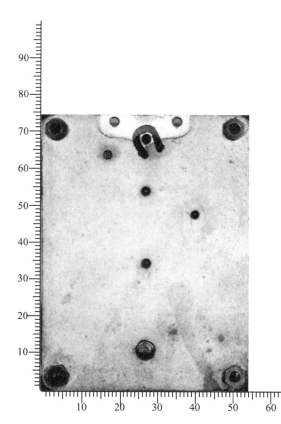

Badische Standard, 30 day
Rectangular
55 x 75 x 24mm

Notes
Lantern pinions. Loop-end mainspring.

Due to variations in bobs, you may have to use blocks and wires other than those shown. The 3-ball bob uses the wire shown and the medium bottom block

Most clocks have horizontal adjustable arms. This one is almost vertical.

The loop end spring showing beneath the plates.

Rapid Recognition Tips
Look for the distinctive upward angle of the adjustable arm and the rounded corners.

The open spring showing beneath the plates indicates that this is not a 400 day movement.

Data
Movement ID Code **AH-30**
Plate shape .... **Rectangular**
Plate width **55mm**
Plate height **75mm**
Gap between plates **24mm**
Escapement type .... **Pin pallet**
Original key size **3.25mm**
Winding side .... **Central, front**
Pivot adjuster .... **Adjustable arm**
Locking device: .... **None**
Pendulum type/s **3-ball**
Mainspring barrel .... **n/a**
Replacement wire .... **No. 12 (Horolovar™ 0.0032"/0.081mm)**
Replacement unit .... **None, you must assemble your own**
Jig settings **98mm, 110mm**
Mainspring .... **Loop end 8mm x 0.3 x 400mm**
Beats per minute **8**
Bob weight .... **395g.**

Examples of clocks fitted with the Badische Uhrenfabrik/Huber 30 day movement

Edgar Henn

Edgar Henn was not a prolific manufacturer of clocks, and the majority of examples have no name, or carry the name of an importer.

Typical importer's names on the backplate:
Euramca
Forrestville

Edgar Henn listings:

By model:

By Movement Identity Code:

By dimensions:
Rectangular

Manufacturer:
Edgar Henn

Model:
Henn Standard narrow
43mm x 94mm x 33mm
(excluding side extensions)

Backplate information:
No (0) Jewels
4 (Four) Jewels
Unadjusted
Made in Germany
May have
Euramca Trading Corp or
Forestville

Movement ID code: **EH-SN**

Notes:
A small bracket screwed to the backplate allows the eccentric nut to be replaced if necessary. Two models exist, one with no jewels and one with the escape wheel and pallet arbors both jewelled. Side plate extensions are fitted to increase the apparent width of the plates.

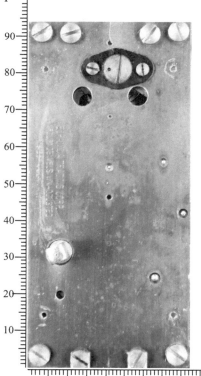

With the side extensions in place

Henn Standard narrow
43 x 94 x 33mm (excluding side extensions)

Notes
Due to an outdated import regulation, clocks with plates less than about 45mm (1.77") wide could enter the USA as watches as opposed to clocks, attracting a lower rate of import duty.

Edgar Henn produced a narrow movement with two detachable plate extensions which was imported at the watch tariff. Prior to sale, the plate extensions were fitted, giving the appearance of a standard and therefore more up-market movement.

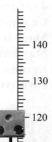

One of the side extensions fitted

Rapid Recognition Tips
The steel bracket that holds the eccentric nut in place is unique to this movement.
The pendulum cup in the base has a square hole to prevent rotation when locked.

Data
Movement ID code .... **EH-SN**
Plate shape .... **Rectangular**
Plate width **43mm**
Plate height **94mm**
Gap between plates **33mm**
Escapement type .... **Dead beat**
Original key size **4.50mm**
Winding side .... **Left**
Pivot adjuster.............. **Eccentric nut**
Locking device: .... **Beneath the base**
Pendulum type/s **4-ball**
Mainspring barrel .... **23mm x 41mm**
Replacement wire .... **No. 17 (Horolovar™ 0.0037"/0.094mm)**
Replacement unit .... **EH-S (Horolovar™ 32)**
Jig settings **110mm, 115mm**
Mainspring .... **19 x 0.40 x 38mm (1350mm)**
Beats per minute **8**
Bob weight .... **290g.**

Examples of clocks fitted with the Henn Standard narrow movement

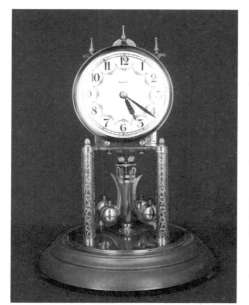 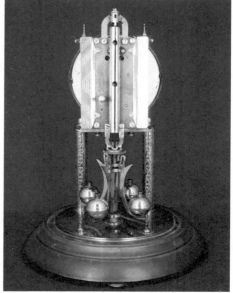

Manufacturer:
Edgar Henn

Model:
Henn Miniature
43mm x 75mm x 30mm

Backplate information:
Normally unmarked
May have an importer's name

Movement ID code: **EH-MIN**

Notes:
Top corners are rounded and the plates are screwed together. The pendulum illustrated uses a rather inefficient system of weights sliding in eccentric grooves on a flat disk.

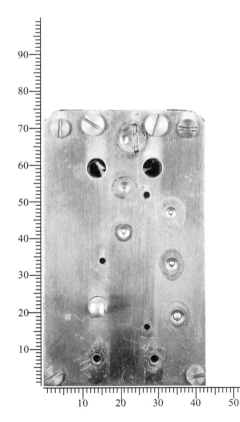

Henn Miniature
43 x 75x 30mm

Notes
The front plates have inspection holes.
Dials often fitted with knurled nuts, not
pins.

Rapid Recognition Tips
The pendulum cup in the base has a large
square hole to prevent rotation when locked.

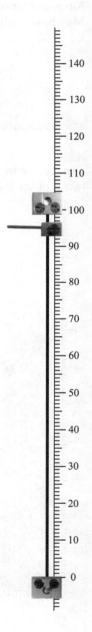

Data
Movement ID code	**EH-MIN**
Plate shape	**Rectangular**
Plate width	**43mm**
Plate height	**75mm**
Gap between plates	**30mm**
Escapement type	**Dead beat**
Original key size	**3.75mm**
Winding side	**Left**
Pivot adjuster	**Eccentric nut**
Locking device:	**Beneath the base**
Pendulum type/s	**4-ball**
Mainspring barrel	**22mm x 35mm**
Replacement wire	**No. 6 (Horolovar™ 0.0023"/0.058mm)**
Replacement unit	**EH-MN (Horolovar™ 29B**
Jig settings	**95mm, 99mm**
Mainspring	**19 x 0.40 x 32mm (951mm)**
Beats per minute	**8**
Bob weight	**210g.**

Examples of clocks fitted with the Henn Miniature movement

 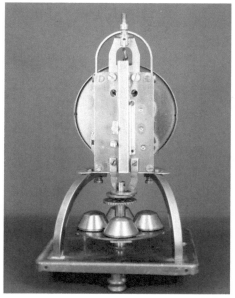

Franz Hermle & Söhne

Franz Hermle movements normally carry the FHS logo.

Although it was a large factory, and they made large numbers of conventional clocks, the range of Anniversary clock movements was limited.

They still manufacture mechanical movements.

Franz Hermle listings:

By model:

By Movement Identity Code:

By dimensions:

Manufacturer:
Franz Hermle & Söhne

Model:
Hermle Standard
69mm x 93mm x 30mm

Backplate information:
May have:
FHS
Germany
with or without a clock showing 7:23

Movement ID code: **FH-STD**

Notes:
This model is distinctive by the two large bevelled inspection holes and the horizontal screwed bracket that adjusts the pivot position. However, other movements can have bevelled inspection holes.

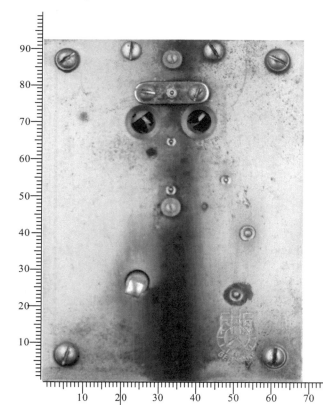

Hermle Standard
69 x 93 x 30mm

Notes

Rapid Recognition Tips

The horizontal screwed bracket that acts as pivot adjuster is unique to this model.

Pivot adjuster and inspection holes

Data

Movement ID code	**FH-STD**
Plate shape	**Rectangular**
Plate width	**69mm**
Plate height	**93mm**
Gap between plates	**30mm**
Escapement type	**Dead beat**
Original key size...........	**4.00mm**
Winding side	**Left**
Pivot adjuster..............	**Screwed bracket**
Locking device:	**On the guard**
Pendulum type/s	**4-ball**
Mainspring barrel	**22mm x 43mm**
Replacement wire	**No. 13 (Horolovar™ 0.0033"/0.084mm)**
Replacement unit	**FH-S (Horolovar™ 25A)**
Jig settings	**92mm, 100mm**
Mainspring	**18 x 0.45 x 38mm (1120mm)**
Beats per minute	**8**
Bob weight	**215g.**

Examples of clocks fitted with the Hermle standard movement

Manufacturer:
Franz Hermle & Söhne

Model:
Hermle Miniature
43mm x 65mm x 21mm

Backplate information:
May have:
FHS Germany
on a clock face showing 7:23

Movement ID code: **FH-MIN**

Notes:
This model is distinctive by the triangular shaped backplate which has a curved top with a large cut out.
The plates are 43mm wide at the base, reducing to 35mm at the top. 65mm high at the centre.

Hermle Miniature
43 x 65 x 21mm (max)

Notes

The top block of a Hermle miniature unit has a small arc cut out of the lower edge. This can be filed out of a standard block with a round needle file, and some ready-made units may also need modification.

Rapid Recognition Tips

If the plates are triangular with a curved top, it was made by Franz Hermle & Söhne.

Data

Movement ID code	**FH-MIN**
Plate shape	**Triangular**
Plate width	**43mm**
Plate height	**65mm**
Gap between plates	**21mm**
Escapement type	**Dead beat**
Original key size...........	**4.00mm**
Winding side	**Left**
Pivot adjuster...............	**Screwed bracket**
Locking device:	**Beneath the base**
Pendulum type/s	**4-ball**
Mainspring barrel	**15mm x 32mm**
Replacement wire	**No. 5 (Horolovar™ 0.0022"/0.056mm)**
Replacement unit	**FH-M (Horolovar™ 25B)**
Jig settings	**79mm, 84mm**
Mainspring	**13 x 0.35 x 30mm (970mm)**
Beats per minute	**8**
Bob weight	**170g.**

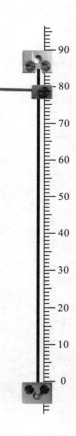

Examples of clocks fitted with the Hermle Miniature movement

Franz Vosseler

Franz Vosseler made a small number of Anniversary
Clocks, mostly with round plates.

Franz Vosseler listings:

Manufacturer:

Franz Vosseler

Model:

Vosseler small
60mm diameter

Backplate information:

Fr. Vosseler or unmarked.

Movement ID code: **FV-60**

Notes:

Circular movement of 60mm diameter with a cutout in the top. 30 day duration. The suspension is held by a bracket riveted to the backplate. The fork is pinned to the suspension wire.

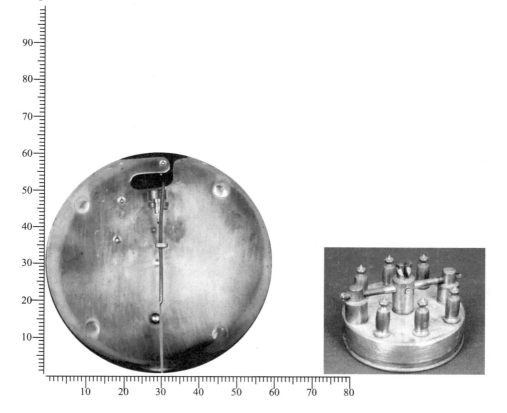

Vosseler small
60mm diameter

The front-plate.

Notes

This is a lunar (30 day) movement.
The movement is sometimes inside a drum suspended from the top of the case.
The suspension is pinned into the blocks and fork. The verge pin passes through the slot in the fork on the backplate, which twists the suspension wire.
To remove the movement from the drum, pull off the hand shaft bush. The dial and motion work will separate from the movement.

The pinned unit parts

Rapid Recognition Tips

Round movement with distinctive cutout at top.
Loop end mainspring. American style verge escapement.
Front wind.

Data

Movement ID Code **FV-60**
Plate shape .... **Round**
Plate width **60mm**
Plate height **60mm**
Gap between plates **15mm**
Escapement type .... **American style verge**
Original key size .... **2.50mm.**
Winding side .... **Central**
Pivot adjuster .... **Adjustable arm**
Locking device: .... **None**
Pendulum type/s .... **Disc, 3 ball**
Mainspring barrel .... **Loop end**
Replacement wire .... **No.10 (Horolovar™ 0.003"/0.076mm)**
Replacement unit .... **None**
Jig settings **8mm, 100mm**
Mainspring .... **7mm x 0.40mm x 600mm**
Beats per minute **10**
Bob weight .... **180g.**

Examples of clocks fitted with the Vosseler 60mm diameter movement.

Gebrüder Junghans Uhrenfabrik

Gebrüder Junghans is best known by the distinctive 'Shield' model, marked with just a serial number. Earlier ones had a plain round bezel.

Junghans was a major manufacturer of conventional mechanical clock movements, and went on to produce a huge range of quartz and radio-controlled clocks and watches. Their famous logo of a J within a star does not appear on the shield clock.

In 1925 they acquired Gustav Becker.

Gebrüder Junghans Uhrenfabrik listings:

Manufacturer:
Gebrüder Junghans Uhrenfabrik

Model:
Junghans Circular 90mm diameter

Backplate information:
Normally only marked with a serial number

The top block cannot be rotated. To adjust the beat you need to twist the wire slightly, as close to the top block as possible.

Movement ID code: **GJ-90**

Notes:

Circular movement of 90mm diameter with a large cutout in the top.

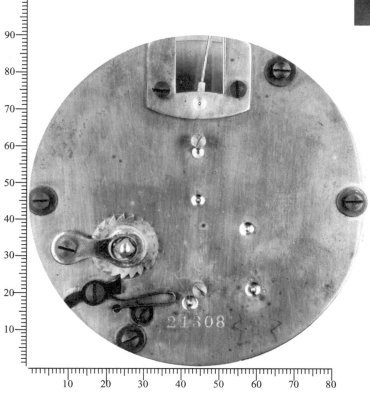

Junghans Shield
90mm diameter

Shield dial

Notes

A tubular suspension guard is mounted on two brass spacers.

The pendulum bob has a silvered scale with two adjustable balls. The dial is normally silvered with black numerals. The disc bob has a silvered band around the circumference, which is difficult to reproduce when restoring.

The base has sharp edges and can scratch a polished surface.

You can use an inverted bottom block if the original top block is missing.

Rapid Recognition Tips

Normally used with the distinctive shield dial.

The disc pendulum with two balls is unique to Junghans.

The Junghans disc pendulum with adjustable balls

Data

Movement ID Code **GJ-90**
Plate shape .... **Round**
Plate width **90mm**
Plate height **90mm**
Gap between plates **31mm**
Escapement type .... **Dead beat**
Original key size .... **3.75mm.**
Winding side .... **Left**
Pivot adjuster .... **Screwed bracket**
Locking device: .... **None**
Pendulum type/s .... **Disc with 2 balls**
Mainspring barrel .... **23mm x 40mm**
Replacement wire .... **No.19 (Horolovar™ 0.004"/0.102mm)**
Replacement unit .... **None**
Jig settings **110, 125mm**
Mainspring .... **19 x 0.45x 36mm (1140mm)**
Beats per minute **8**
Bob weight .... **375g.**

Georg Würthner

Würthner was not a prolific manufacturer of Anniversary clocks. While some bear the name in text, others are unmarked or have the name of an importer.

The script logo often seen on the dials of Würthner clocks.

Georg Würthner listings:

Manufacturer:
Georg Würthner

Model:
Würthner   Western   Standard   Narrow
42mm x 93mm x 30mm

Backplate information:
NO (0) JEWELS
UNADJUSTED
MADE IN GERMANY
WURTHNER WESTERN GERMANY

Movement ID code: **GW-SN**

Notes:

Würthner Western Standard Narrow
44 x 70 x 23mm

Notes

The typical flat wire click spring normally found on Würthner clocks.

Rapid Recognition Tips

Look for the unusual flat wire click on most Würthner movements. Held in place by the head of a plate screw, it wraps around a brass screw and then bends back under the click.

Data

Movement ID Code	**GW-SN**
Plate shape	**Rectangular**
Plate width	**42mm**
Plate height	**93mm**
Gap between plates	**30mm**
Escapement type	**Dead Beat**
Original key size	**4.00mm**
Winding side	**Left**
Pivot adjuster	**Eccentric nut**
Locking device:	**None**
Pendulum type/s	**4-ball**
Mainspring barrel	**22mm x 39mm**
Replacement wire	**No. 9 (Horolovar™ 0.004"/0.102mm)**
Replacement unit	**GW-S (Horolovar™ 26)**
Jig settings	**104mm, 112mm**
Mainspring	**19 x 0.45 x 36mm (1140mm)**
Beats per minute	**8**
Bob weight	**300g.**

140
130
120
110
100
90
80
70
60
50
40
30
20
10
0

Examples of clocks fitted with the Würthner Standard Narrow movement

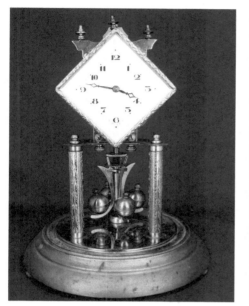

Gerson Wintermantel & Cie

Prior to the formation of the Jahresuhrenfabrik Schatz factory by G. Wintermantel & A. Schatz, 400 day clocks were made by a small group known as Gerson Wintermantel & Cie.

Gerson Wintermantel worked with August Schatz, making 400 day clocks in the early 1880's, and in conjunction with Anton Harder's patents, produced a basic format that was to remain fundamental to almost all 400 day clock designs until mass production ceased 100 years later.

A surprising number of these early clocks have survived, but within a few years the company was reorganised into Jahresuhren-fabrik A.G., so not many clocks were made.

Early examples bear the mark GW&Cie plus a serial number with the letter R on the backplate, and although this was soon dropped, the letter R continued to be stamped near the serial number.

The group was also known by the letters WC.

Gerson Wintermantel listings:

By model:

By Movement Identity Code:

By plate dimensions:

Rectangular

These early Gerson Wintermantel & Cie. clocks should not be confused with the much later Wintermantel Uhrenfabrik clocks, described later in this book.

Manufacturer:
Gersen Wintermantel & Cie

Model:
Gerson Wintermantel Standard
67mm x 88mm x 30mm

Backplate information:
**Normally only marked with a serial
number and the letter R.
Early models marked GW&Cie**

Movement ID code: **WC-STD**

Notes:
Rectangular movement with a low serial
number and the letter R.

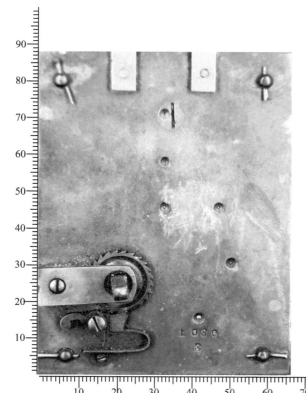

*The later dial with the word
'Patent' 3 times. Earlier dials
mention the Harder patent.*

The first dials bore the words
Harder Ranson bei Steinau a/O.
In 1880 *D.R. PATENT No. 2437*
was added and about 3 years later
the dial was changed to show just
the three patent numbers
abbreviated to:
DRP2437 LLP2182 USP269052.

This was promptly changed to
*D. R. PATENT 2437 L.L.PATENT
2182 U.S.PATENT 269052* as
shown above.

Gerson Wintermantel Standard
67 x 88 x 30mm

Notes
These clocks were made in small numbers.
They have shorter pillars than the subsequent
Jahresuhrenfabrik clocks, at about 75mm
between the base and the platform.
However, the very first Jahresuhrenfabrik clocks
also had short pillars.

The top block with the retaining screw that tends to dig into the block

The top block was held in place by a single screw on early models, which
had the disadvantage of digging into the block. This hindered subsequent
adjustment, as the screw would want to locate in the hole its point had
made in the block previously. You will see clocks with a second hole on
the other side of the bracket.

Rapid Recognition Tips
Small white dials with varying patent text in
a circle.
The disc pendulums are generally very thin.

Data
Movement ID Code	**WC-STD**
Plate shape	**Rectangular**
Plate width	**67mm**
Plate height	**88mm**
Gap between plates	**30mm**
Escapement type	**Dead beat**
Original key size	**4.25mm.**
Winding side	**Left**
Pivot adjuster	**Eccentric nut**
Locking device:	**None**
Pendulum type/s	**Disc**
Mainspring barrel	**22mm x 40mm**
Replacement wire	**No.19 (Horolovar™ 0.004"/0.102mm)**
Replacement unit	**None**
Jig settings	**105, n/a**
Mainspring	**19 x 0.45x 36mm (1140mm)**
Beats per minute	**8**
Bob weight	**300g.**

Examples of clocks fitted with the Gerson Wintermantel movement

Grivolas

The only French mass producer of 400 Day Clocks, Grivolas made very fine and elegant clocks. However, two types of Grivolas exist:

- Those with very high quality movements made in France
- Less expensive models fitted with movements from Germany.

There is nothing unauthentic about a 'German Grivolas'. They were not made from married-up parts by unscrupulous vendors. The high cost of the clocks with French movements made them less easy to sell, and the company simply fitted German movements to their cheaper range of clocks.

Identifying the two types is simple: if it is **Front-wind**, it is **French**.

Grivolas listings:

Notes:

Grivolas movements, whether French or German, are fitted to their bezels with a twisting action, and locked in place with a screw through the bottom of the bezel. To remove the movement, carefully undo the retaining screw while holding the movement in case it falls. If the retaining pegs are missing it can fall out.

Gently rotate the movement a few degrees until the pegs in the bezel line up with the slots in the dial. With careful jiggling the movement can be withdrawn.

If you force it, you may damage the enamel dial.

Notches for the dial retaining pins in the bezel

Manufacturer:
Grivolas

Model:
Grivolas French
110mm x 30mm

Backplate information:
PENDULES 400 JOURS
PARIS
FABRICATION FRANÇAISE
The number following the single
letter on the backplate indicates the
year of manufacture. This clock has
C-13, so was made in 1913.

Movement ID code: **GR-FR**

Notes:

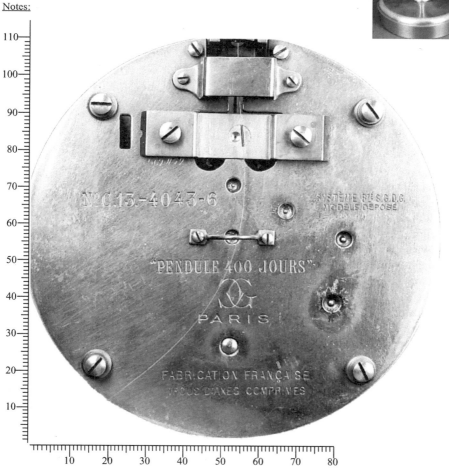

Grivolas French
110mm x 30mm

The complex top block, similar to the Hauck design.

Notes
This delicate movement was manufactured with the same quality and precision as the finest conventional French movements.
The pendulums have their weights concealed inside the bob, with an adjuster hole in the side. This can give the illusion of a stationary pendulum from a distance.

The bob adjuster.

No ready made replacement unit is available, due to the top block arrangement. The fork and bottom block can be replaced with standard items if necessary, but the original bottom block had a shapely top.

Rapid Recognition Tips
The only round, front-wind 400 day movement.

Inside the bob.

Data
Movement ID code .... **GR-FR**
Plate shape .... **Round**
Plate width **110mm**
Plate height **110mm**
Gap between plates **30mm**
Escapement type .... **Dead beat**
Original key size **3.25mm**
Winding side .... **Central**
Pivot adjuster .... **Eccentric nut**
Locking device: .... **None**
Pendulum type/s .... **Disc**
Mainspring barrel .... **23mm x 48mm**
Replacement wire .... **No. 20 (Horolovar™ 0.004"/0.102mm)**
Replacement unit .... **None**
Jig settings **121mm, 125mm**
Mainspring .... **20 x 0.40 x 45mm (2030mm)**
Beats per minute **8**
Bob weight .... **325g.**

The underside of the bob.

Examples of clocks fitted with the Grivolas French movement

Manufacturer:

Grivolas

Model:

**Grivolas German
67mm x 87mm x 30mm**

Backplate information:

**May have
DRP No. 144688
USP No. 751686
May have a serial number
They may be a number stamped on the edge of
the backplate which may also be written under
the pendulum.**

*Serial number and star stamped on
the edge of the back plate.*

Movement ID code: **GR-DE**

Notes:

Movement manufactured in Germany by P.
Hauck. The bottom corners of the front plate
were rounded off to make it fit the Grivolas
bezel.

*Serial number of the movement
manufacturer and the Grivolas
number, written under the
pendulum..*

Grivolas German
67 x 87x 30mm

Notes

This movement is similar to the movement described in the P. Hauck section.

It was not made specially for Grivolas - the front plate has holes threaded for a nonexistent pediment, and the front plate lower corners appear to have been curved after production and the area re-lacquered. No top block readily available.

Because the movement was not made by Grivolas, the dial is almost certain to have their name and logo. Movements were also bought from Jahresuhrenfabrik.

Rapid Recognition Tips

A Grivolas with rear wind will have a German movement.

Back plate lower corners rounded off by Grivolas.

Data

Movement ID code	**GR-DE**
Plate shape	**Rectangular**
Plate width	**67mm**
Plate height	**87mm**
Gap between plates	**30mm**
Escapement type	**Dead beat**
Original key size	**4.00mm**
Winding side	**Left**
Pivot adjuster..............	**Eccentric nut**
Locking device:	**None**
Pendulum type/s	**Disc**
Mainspring barrel	**23mm x 39mm**
Replacement wire	**No. 18 (Horolovar™ 0.0038"/0.097mm)**
Replacement unit	**Not readily available**
Jig settings	**114mm, 123mm**
Mainspring	**19 x 0.45 x 36mm (1140mm)**
Beats per minute	**8**
Bob weight	**390g.**

Examples of clocks fitted with the Grivolas German movement

Gustav Becker

Gustav Becker was one of the best known makers of early Anniversary Clocks, and their factory produced a vast number of very high quality clocks of all types.

Their Anniversary clocks used the same basic movement, but the styles and the upper suspension brackets varied considerably.

Most examples carry the distinctive logos.
The firm was bought by Junghans in 1925.

Gustav Becker listings:

By model:
Becker Standard 69mm x 93mm x 30mm   9-3

By Movement Identity Code:
GB-STD Becker Standard   9-3

By dimensions:
Rectangular
69mm x 93mm x 30mm Becker Standard   9-3

Dating by serial number.

The majority of Gustav Becker clocks carried a serial number, and the factory records, kindly given to me by the late Karl Kochmann, show the numbers in use at various times. However, these numbers only relate to the Freiburg factory and there is some doubt over their accuracy as new information comes to light. A new factory was opened at Braunau in about 1888, and the numbers began at 1. Junghans bought the business in 1925, and used a fresh range of serial numbers until they abandoned them. According to Karl Kochmann, the records of numbers used after 1926 were lost during the second world war. In order to date a <u>400 day</u> clock by the serial number, the table below is likely to give the right answer in most cases.

Year	Serial No		
1850	480	1885	500,000
1860	4000	1890	800,000
1863	10,000	1892	1,000,000
1865	15,000	1900	1,500,000
1867	25,000	1913	1,850,000
1872	50,000	1923	1,860,000
1875	100,000	1925	1,945,399
1880	260,000	1926	2,244,868

Manufacturer:
Gustav Becker

Model:
Becker Standard
69mm x 93mm x 30mm

Backplate information:
**Distinctive anchor marked GB, often
inside a circle. May have:
GB Anchor
Medaille d'or
Serial number**

Movement ID code: **GB-STD**

Notes:
Most examples bear the Medaille d'Or (Gold Medal) logo in addition to the anchor. Many
of these clocks can be dated by the serial number.

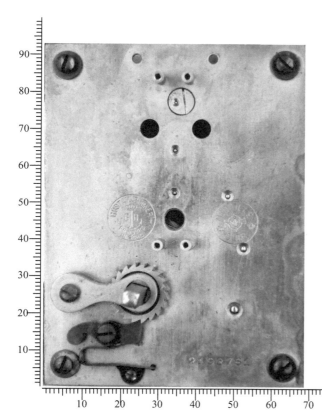

*The less common Becker 4-
ball pendulum*

Becker Standard
69 x 93 x 30mm

Simple adjuster

Notes
Almost every example has an unused hole in the centre of the plates.

These fine clocks can be found with simple suspension supports and with complex indexed adjusters to facilitate setting in beat. *For this reason, no reliable suspension information can be provided.* Later models have a flat suspension guard screwed to two pairs of spacers, which also acts as a basic locking device.

Indexed adjuster

Rapid Recognition Tips
The pairs of pillars on which the flat guard was mounted are unique to Gustav Becker.

Data
Movement ID Code ...... **GB-STD**
Plate shape .... **Rectangular**
Plate width **69mm**
Plate height **93mm**
Gap between plates **30mm**
Escapement type .... **Dead beat**
Original key size .... **4.00mm & 2mm.**
Winding side .... **Left**
Pivot adjuster .... **Eccentric nut**
Locking device: .... **Guard slider**
Pendulum type/s .... **Disc, 4-ball**
Mainspring barrel .... **23mm x 41mm**
Replacement wire .... **No.19 (Horolovar™ 0.004"/0.102mm)**
Replacement unit .... **None**
Jig settings **12mm, 124mm**
Mainspring .... **19 x 0.40 x 38mm (1350mm)**
Beats per minute **8**
Bob weight .... **425g.**

The typical Gustav Becker guard pillars.
If you remove them, be sure to put the ones with the longer screws back in the top holes or they may touch the barrel.

Examples of clocks fitted with Gustav Becker movements

Hettich

Hettich was famous for inventing the floating balance. It proved very successful, and the portability of these clocks removed most of the problems that pendulum clocks suffered from when repositioned or moved for cleaning.

The story goes that the German courts awarded Hettich huge compensation when other factories copied his patented designs without permission. The compensation was so large that the Hettich family no longer needed to work and closed the firm.

Hettich listings:

Manufacturer:
Hettich

Model:
Hettich Remontoire
44mm x 40mm x 19mm

Backplate information:
**HETTICH
GERMANY
ONE (1) JEWEL
UNADJUSTED**

Movement ID code: **HE-REM**

Notes:
Derived from an original design that used a large horizontal balance wheel.
Above the movement is a large battery holder. The pendulum weights have individual adjustment screws for regulation.

The balls have individual adjustment screws.

Hettich Remontoire
44 x 40 x 19mm

Notes
Although battery powered, it is in fact a weight driven movement. A falling weight on an arm provides the energy to drive the clock. As the weight approaches the bottom, electrical contacts are made and a solenoid kicks the weight back up again.

As the beats of this clock are fairly fast (60bpm), a small spring is used to maintain power to the movement while the weight is being kicked back up, similar to the 'maintaining power' found in many regulators.

The pendulum uses Hettich's ingenious 'Floating Balance' design

Rapid Recognition Tips
Large solenoid and battery holder.
Rapid pendulum rotation.
Coiled spring around the pendulum rod.
Most examples have a seconds hand.

When the weight on the arm reaches the bottom, a contact is made which energizes the coil above, which kicks the weight back up again.

Data

Movement ID Code	**HE-REM**
Plate shape	**Rectangular**
Plate width	**44mm**
Plate height	**40mm**
Gap between plates	**19mm**
Escapement type	**Pin Pallet**
Original Battery	**1.5v D cell**
Winding side	**N/A**
Pivot adjuster	**N/A**
Locking device:	**None**
Pendulum type/s	**4-ball**
Mainspring barrel	**N/A**
Replacement wire	**N/A**
Replacement unit	**N/A**
Jig settings	**N/A**
Mainspring	**N/A**
Beats per minute	**60**
Bob weight	**N/A**

Examples of clocks fitted with Hettich movements

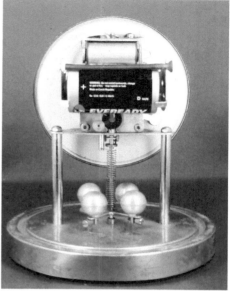

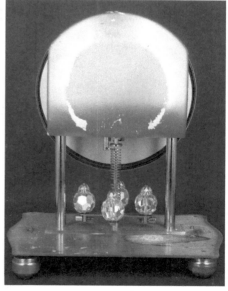

Jahresuhrenfabrik
A. Schatz & Söhne

The Jahresuhrenfabrik company, also known by its much shorter name of Schatz after the founder Aug. Schatz, made vast numbers of Anniversary clocks from the turn of the century onwards. Fortunately, for the purposes of identification, the majority of later examples carry distinctive logos with a model number. Conversely, the early examples normally have no marks other than perhaps a serial number or Germany.

The famous 'Elephant' logo found on many pre and post war examples.

Identification of later models normally requires little less than to find the model number such as 49, 53, 54 etc. in the model table below. Examples prior to the 1st world war will need further investigation by comparing models with plates of the same dimensions.

One of the many model number stamps used. Others include 53, 54, 59, BA, JUM/7 & TSM

Jahresuhrenfabrik listings:

By model:

By Movement Identity Code:

By dimensions:

Manufacturer:

Jahresuhrenfabrik
A. Schatz & Söhne

Model:

JUF Standard original
66mm x 88mm x 30mm

Backplate information:

Any of the following, or unmarked
Elephant logo
Made in Germany
Patent Angemeldet
Patents Applied
DRP No. 144688

Movement ID code: **JS-SO**

Notes:

This is the earliest of their standard movements, with slightly thicker plates and a one piece ratchet wheel bracket. Patent Angemeldet/Patents Applied appeared until the DRP (Deutsche Republik Patent) No. 144688 was granted. The patent was for a compensating pendulum but the number also appears on clocks not originally fitted with the pendulum.

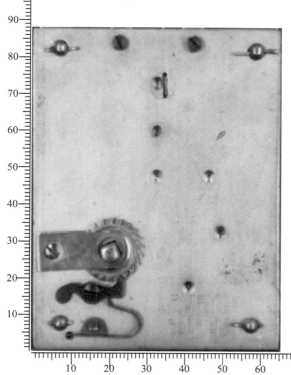

JUF Standard original
66 x 88 x 30mm

Notes

The front plate was normally screwed to the pillars, with large steel washers. The plates were slightly thicker than later models, at 2.4mm.

On the next page is an example bearing the Badische Uhrenfabrik logo on the frontplate, but it is highly unlikely that they were the manufacturers. In fact they purchased movements from JUF Schatz.

Prior to the formation of Jahresuhrenfabrik Schatz, very similar clocks were made by Gerson Wintermantel with whom August Schatz was in business.

The suspension illustrated fits a large number of examples but by no means all of them. The very early examples were quite short.

Rapid Recognition Tips

The ratchet wheel support is made from one piece, like those by Philip Hauck, but horizontal.

Data

Movement ID Code ...... **JS-SO**
Plate shape .... **Rectangular**
Plate width **66mm**
Plate height **88mm**
Gap between plates **30mm**
Escapement type .... **Dead beat**
Original key size **4.00mm**
Winding side .... **Left**
Pivot adjuster .... **Eccentric nut**
Locking device: .... **Optionally on the guard**
Pendulum type/s .... **Disc, 4-ball**
Mainspring barrel .... **22.7mm x 40mm**
Replacement wire .... **No.20 (Horolovar™ 0.004"/0.102mm)**
Replacement unit .... **JS-S (Horolovar™ 6789)**
Jig settings **108mm, 114mm**
Mainspring .... **19 x 0.45 x 36mm (1140mm)**
Beats per minute **8**
Bob weight .... **370/380g.**

Examples of clocks fitted with the Jahresuhrenfabrik Standard Original movement

Manufacturer:
Jahresuhrenfabrik
A. Schatz & Söhne

Model:
JUF Standard early
66mm x 88mm x 30mm

Backplate information:
Any of the following, or unmarked
Jahresuhrenfabrik G.m.b.H Germany
Elephant logo
Made in Germany
A serial number

Movement ID code: **JS-SE**

Notes:

To avoid confusion, this movement has been shown on a separate page to the later 49 model. The plates are slightly different but in general terms the movements are the same. This version has no inspection holes and may or may not have guard screws.

There is often a letter or mark here in the corner such as D, F or R on early models.

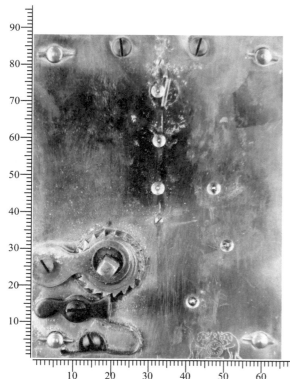

JUF Standard early
66 x 88 x 30mm

Early bracket   *Swivel bracket*

Notes

Several types of suspension bracket were used. The earlier one had the block above the bracket. Later models had the block support beneath the bracket. Others had an easily rotated bracket.

It is common to see the guard screw-holes as just dots on earlier models.

The jig settings shown are for the later bracket. For the earlier model, the fork needs to be lowered by about 4mm. The ready-made units will not suit the swivel bracket.

Later bracket

Rapid Recognition Tips

1: Many examples have two undrilled dots where the suspension guard screws were to go on later models. The top hole is just above the eccentric nut.

2: Often a gap between platform and plates on later models.

Typical gap between the platform and the plates on later models.

Data

Movement ID Code	**JS-SE**
Plate shape	**Rectangular**
Plate width	**66mm**
Plate height	**88mm**
Gap between plates	**30mm**
Escapement type	**Dead beat**
Original key size	**4.00mm**
Winding side	**Left**
Pivot adjuster	**Eccentric nut**
Locking device:	**Optionally on the guard**
Pendulum type/s	**Disc, 4-ball**
Mainspring barrel	**22.7mm x 40mm**
Replacement wire	**No.20 (Horolovar™ 0.004"/0.102mm)**
Replacement unit	**JS-S (Horolovar™ 6789)**
Jig settings	**107mm, 114mm**
Mainspring	**19 x 0.45 x 36mm (1140mm)**
Beats per minute	**8**
Bob weight	**370/380g.**

Examples of clocks fitted with the Jahresuhrenfabrik Standard Early movement

Examples of clocks fitted with the Jahresuhrenfabrik Standard Early movement

Manufacturer:
Jahresuhrenfabrik
A. Schatz & Söhne

Model:
JUF Standard 49
66mm x 88mm x 30mm

Backplate information:
May be unmarked or have
Schatz & Söhne 49 Germany
Jahresuhrenfabrik 49 Germany
Made in Germany

Movement ID code: **JS-S49**

Notes:
To avoid confusion this movement has been shown on a separate page to the earlier model. The backplate is slightly different but in general terms it is the same movement. This plate has inspection holes and guard screws.

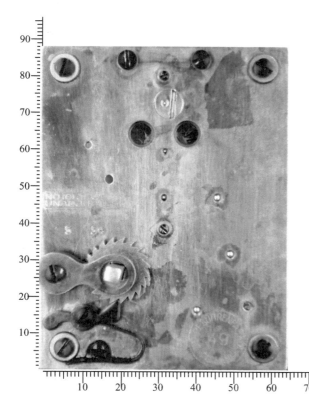 

JUF Standard 49
66 x 88 x 30mm

Notes

Many features of this later model were copied by other factories when the patents expired, making it more difficult to positively identify at first glance. Uhrenfabrik Herr & Reiner made a very similar movement.

The rare watch spring & barrel where a wheel would normally be.

A very small quantity had a watch mainspring fitted in a barrel in place of one of the wheels. It is not clear what purpose this served. Some say it was to assist the clock during the final weeks of the year. Others think it was to even out the pressure on the escapement should the mainspring stick.

Whatever its purpose, it did not seem to do the job well and the idea was soon abandoned, probably due to the cost.

Rapid Recognition Tips

1: Normally a gap between the platform and the plates on later models, however others also introduced gaps.

2: The logo bearing the number 49 is unique to this movement.

Typical gap between the platform and the plates.

Data

Movement ID Code **JS-S49**
Plate shape .... **Rectangular**
Plate width **66mm**
Plate height **88mm**
Gap between plates **30mm**
Escapement type .... **Dead beat**
Original key size **4.00mm**
Winding side .... **Left**
Pivot adjuster .... **Eccentric nut**
Locking device: .... **Optionally on the guard**
Pendulum type/s .... **Disc, 4-ball**
Mainspring barrel .... **22.7mm x 40mm**
Replacement wire .... **No.20 (Horolovar™ 0.004"/0.102mm)**
Replacement unit .... **JS-S (Horolovar™ 6789)**
Jig settings **107mm, 114mm**
Mainspring .... **19 x 0.45 x 36mm (1140mm)**
Beats per minute **8**
Bob weight .... **370/380g.**

Examples of clocks fitted with the Jahresuhrenfabrik Schatz Standard 49 movement

Examples of clocks fitted with the Jahresuhrenfabrik Schatz Standard 49 movement

Manufacturer:

Jahresuhrenfabrik
Aug. Schatz & Söhne

Backplate information:

Aug. Schatz & Söhne Germany
JUM/7
Two(2) jewels
Unadjusted

Model:

Schatz Miniature
JUM/7
44mm x 67mm x 21mm

Movement ID code: **JS-JUM7**

Notes:

This movement was widely used, and is one of the most easily identified. It appears in many case styles.

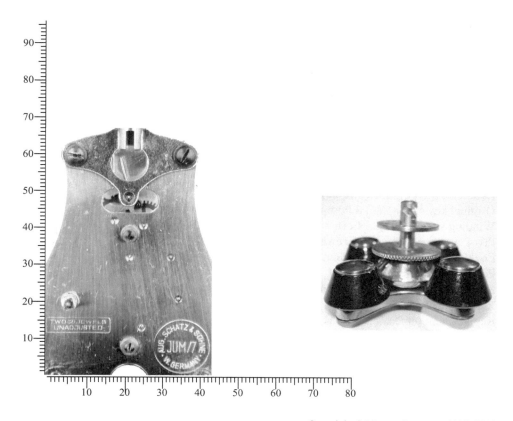

Schatz Miniature JUM/7
44 x 67 x 21mm

The plastic guard

Notes

The month and year of manufacture often appears on the backplate.

The plate dimension shown is the width at the widest point. It is 32mm at the narrowest point. Many examples have a dome with two lugs, which twists to lock in position. The pendulum balls are sprung loaded.

A plastic guard is screwed to the top, a tube covers the suspension and two prongs of the guard lock into the top of the pendulum, making this clock very easy and safe to transport.

Rapid Recognition Tips

The vest shaped plate with JUM/7 is unique to this movement.

Pendulum anti-rotation c

Data

Movement ID Code	**JS-JUM7**
Plate shape	**Vest**
Plate width	**44mm**
Plate height	**67mm**
Gap between plates	**21mm**
Escapement type	**Pin pallet**
Original key size	**3.00mm**
Winding side	**Left**
Pivot adjuster	**Screwed bracket**
Locking device:	**Beneath the base and on the guard**
Pendulum type/s	**4-ball**
Mainspring barrel	**15.7mm x 32.6mm**
Replacement wire	**No. 5 (Horolovar™ 0.0022"/0.056mm)**
Replacement unit	**JS-JM (Horolovar™ 10C)**
Jig settings	**58mm, 63mm**
Mainspring	**13 x 0.35 x 30mm (970mm)**
Beats per minute	**10**
Bob weight	**146g.**

Examples of clocks fitted with the Schatz Miniature JUM/7 movement.

Manufacturer:
Jahresuhrenfabrik
Aug. Schatz & Söhne

Model:
Schatz Miniature 53 vest
44mm x 64mm x 21mm

Backplate information:
Aug. Schatz & Söhne 53 Germany
TWO(2) JEWELS
UNADJUSTED

Movement ID code: **JS-53V**

Notes:
This movement has a conventional backplate, although normally suspended from above.
If the backplate incorporates legs, it is not the same movement.

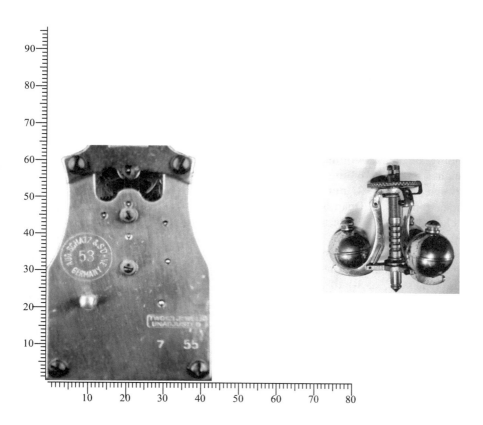

Schatz Miniature 53 vest
44 x 64 x 21mm

Notes

The month and year of manufacture often appears on the backplate.

The movement itself looks similar to the legged version.

Rapid Recognition Tips

Often suspended from above.

Data

Movement ID Code	**JS-53V**
Plate shape	**Vest**
Plate width	**44mm**
Plate height	**64mm**
Gap between plates	**21mm**
Escapement type	**Dead beat**
Original key size	**3.00mm**
Winding side	**Left**
Pivot adjuster	**Screwed bracket**
Locking device:	**On the guard**
Pendulum type/s	**3-ball**
Mainspring barrel	**16mm x 32mm**
Replacement wire	**No. 6 (Horolovar™ 0.0023"/0.058mm)**
Replacement unit	**JS-53 (Horolovar™ 10A)**
Jig settings	**82mm, 87mm**
Mainspring	**13 x 0.35 x 30mm (970mm)**
Beats per minute	**10**
Bob weight	**138g.**

Examples of clocks fitted with the Schatz 53 vest movement

Manufacturer:
Jahresuhrenfabrik
Aug. Schatz & Söhne

Backplate information:
Aug. Schatz & Söhne 53 Germany
Two(2) JEWELS
UNADJUSTED

Model:
Schatz Miniature 53 Legged
44mm x 66mm x 21mm (excluding legs)

Movement ID code: **JS-53L**

Notes:
The movement is similar to the conventional vest shape 53 version, but this one incorporates the pillars as legs in the one-piece plates. The size including legs is 88mm x 120mm.

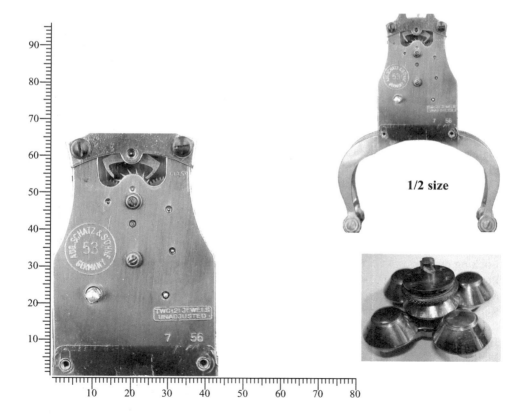

1/2 size

Schatz Miniature 53 Legged
44 x 66 x 21mm (excluding legs)

Notes
This movement normally has a 4-ball pendulum, and the pendulum balls incorporated springs.

The month and year of manufacture often appears on the backplate.

The guard has two prongs which engage into the pendulum, preventing it from turning in transit as well as locking it normally.

Pendulum anti-rotation device

Rapid Recognition Tips
The only movement marked with Schatz 53 in a circle on a plate with curved legs.

Data
Movement ID Code	**JS-53L**
Plate shape	**Legs**
Plate width	**44mm**
Plate height	**64mm**
Gap between plates	**21mm**
Escapement type	**Dead beat**
Original key size	**3.00mm**
Winding side	**Left**
Pivot adjuster	**Screwed bracket**
Locking device:	**On the guard and beneath the base.**
Pendulum type/s	**4-ball**
Mainspring barrel	**16mm x 32mm**
Replacement wire	**No. 6 (Horolovar™ 0.0023"/0.058mm)**
Replacement unit	**JS-53 (Horolovar™ 10A)**
Jig settings	**82mm, 87mm**
Mainspring	**13 x 0.35 x 30mm (970mm)**
Beats per minute	**10**
Bob weight	**172g**

Examples of clocks fitted with the Schatz 53 legged movement

 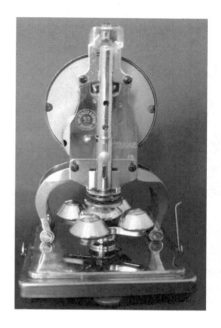

Examples of clocks fitted with the Schatz 53 legged movement

Miniature Schatz movements often had a wall mounting option, but these were not popular and most clocks ended up on a table or shelf. Lantern style cases were very common, and were also made by other firms such as Kern, Kundo & Koma.

This 'Legged' movement was ideal for lantern cases and showed the pendulum well.

These two examples still have their original brackets, probably because they were still in their original packaging. Many brackets were discarded by owners or were an optional extra that didn't sell well.

The lantern model shown here is the 'London Coach' and on its bracket you can see how it got its name.

Manufacturer:

Jahresuhrenfabrik
Aug. Schatz & Söhne

Backplate information:

A Schatz & Sons Germany 54
TWO (2) JEWELS UNADJUSTED
May have RR
May show month & year of
manufacture

Model:

Schatz Miniature 54 1,000 day straight legs
43mm x 66mm x 32mm (excl. legs)

Movement ID code: **JS-54S**

Notes:

By use of a very large spring, this model runs for up to 1,000 days.
Not to be confused with the model that has curved legs.

1/2 size
Straight legs

Schatz Miniature 54 1,000 day
straight legs
43x 66 x 32mm (excluding legs)

Notes
The support legs for this movement and the plates are combined into one piece.
The plate size including legs is 55mm x 130mm.
Two shapes of legs exist: Straight-sided and curved. This is the straight sided leg model.
Some backplates are marked RR, referring to Remington Rand of the USA.

Giant mainspring barrel

Rapid Recognition Tips

1: The mainspring on both models of 1,000 day movements is far bigger than those found on 400 day clocks, .
2: The only movement marked with Schatz 54 in a circle on a plate with straight legs.

Data

Movement ID Code	**JS-54S**
Plate shape	**Legged, straight**
Plate width	**43mm**
Plate height	**70mm**
Gap between plates	**32mm**
Escapement type	**Dead beat**
Original key size	**4.00mm**
Winding side	**Left**
Pivot adjuster	**Screwed bracket**
Locking device:	**Beneath the base**
Pendulum type/s	**4-ball**
Mainspring barrel	**24.5mm x 53mm**
Replacement wire	**No. 7 (Horolovar™ 0.0024"/0.061mm)**
Replacement unit	**JS-54 (Horolovar™ 10B)**
Jig settings	**82mm, 87mm**
Mainspring	**21 x 0.40 x 50mm (2300mm)**
Beats per minute	**10**
Bob weight	**145g.**

Examples of clocks fitted with the Schatz 54 1,000 day straight movement

Manufacturer:
Jahresuhrenfabrik
Aug. Schatz & Söhne

Backplate information:
A Schatz & Sons Germany 54
TWO (2) JEWELS UNADJUSTED
May have RR
May show month & year of
manufacture

Model:
Schatz Miniature 54 1,000 day
curved legs
43mm x 60mm x 32mm (excl. legs)

Movement ID code: **JS-54C**

Notes:
By use of a very large spring, this model runs for up to 1,000 days.
Not to be confused with the model that has straight legs, although the parts are similar.

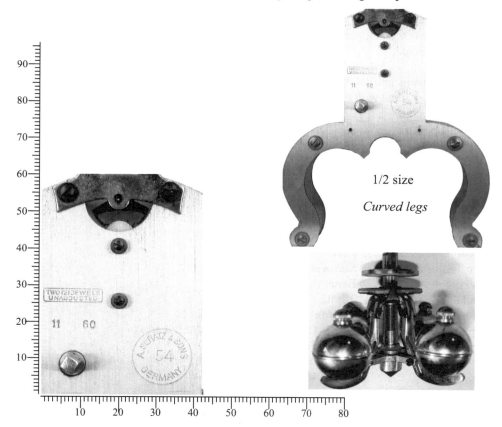

1/2 size

Curved legs

**Schatz Miniature 54 1,000 day
curved legs
43x 60 x 32mm (excluding legs)**

Notes
The support legs for this movement and the plates are combined into one piece.

The plate size including legs is 55mm x 130mm.

Two shapes of legs exist: straight-sided and curved. This is the curved leg model.

The guard has two prongs which locate in holes in the pendulum, preventing it from rotating.

Rapid Recognition Tips
The mainspring is far bigger than those found on 400 day clocks.

The only movement marked with Schatz 54 in a circle on a plate with curved legs.

Data
Movement ID Code **JS-54C**
Plate shape .... **Legged, curved**
Plate width **43mm**
Plate height **70mm**
Gap between plates **32mm**
Escapement type .... **Dead beat**
Original key size **4.00mm**
Winding side .... **Left**
Pivot adjuster .... **Screwed bracket**
Locking device: .... **Beneath the base**
Pendulum type/s **4-ball**
Mainspring barrel .... **24.5mm x 53mm**
Replacement wire .... **No. 7 (Horolovar™ 0.0024"/0.061mm)**
Replacement unit .... **JS-54 (Horolovar™ 10B)**
Jig settings **82mm, 87mm**
Mainspring .... **21 x 0.40 x 50mm (2300mm)**
Beats per minute **10**
Bob weight .... **145g.**

The guard has two prongs which locate in holes in the pendulum

Giant mainspring

Examples of clocks fitted with the Schatz 54 1,000 day curved movement

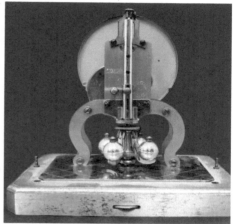

Manufacturer:
Jahresuhrenfabrik
A. Schatz & Söhne

Model:
Schatz Miniature BA Remontoire
44mm x 68mm x 20mm

Backplate information:
A Schatz & Sons Germany BA
TWO (2) JEWELS UNADJUSTED
May show month & year of manufacture

Movement ID code: **JS-BA**

Notes:
Although technically a battery movement, the battery only applies an occasional rewind pulse to maintain mechanical power to the train via a tiny coiled spring.

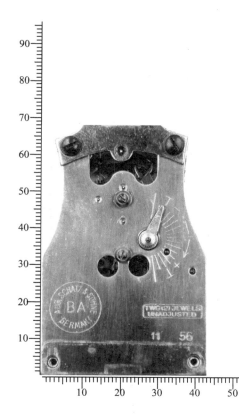

Schatz Miniature BA Remontoire
44x 68 x 20mm

Notes

The battery is mounted beneath the base. 3v 2R10 penlight batteries are currently still made, but can be difficult to obtain. Two AA batteries taped together will operate the clock.

Contact tension adjuster

When you change the battery, take a cotton bud dipped in alcohol and clean the electrical contacts using the holes in the backplate.

The adjuster on the back plate is not for timekeeping. It alters the tension on the electrical contact.

Rapid Recognition Tips

There is no winding shaft.

The only movement marked with Schatz BA in a circle.

Solenoid

Data

Movement ID Code	**JS-BA**
Plate shape	**Vest**
Plate width	**44mm**
Plate height	**68mm**
Gap between plates	**20mm**
Escapement type	**Dead beat**
Battery voltage	**Penlight 3v 2R10**
Winding side	**n/a**
Pivot adjuster	**Screwed bracket**
Locking device:	**Beneath the base**
Pendulum type/s	**3-ball**
Mainspring barrel	**n/a**
Replacement wire	**No. 6 (Horolovar™ 0.0023"/0.058mm)**
Replacement unit	**JS-53 (Horolovar™ 10A)**
Jig settings	**82mm, 87mm**
Mainspring	**n/a**
Beats per minute	**10**
Bob weight	**145g.**

Examples of clocks fitted with the Schatz BA Remontoire movement

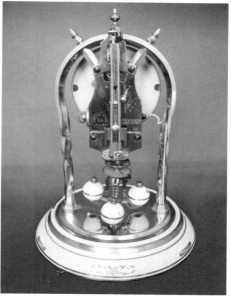

Manufacturer:

**Jahresuhrenfabrik
A. Schatz & Söhne**

Backplate information:

**A Schatz & Sons Germany TSM
No (0) JEWELS UNADJUSTED
May show month & year of
manufacture**

Model:

**Schatz Miniature TSM
Electromagnetic
44mm x 68mm x 20mm**

Movement ID code: **JS-TSM**

Notes:

Although technically a battery movement, this marked the transition from mechanical to electronic movements. Quite the reverse to spring driven and solenoid movements, the battery causes the pendulum to swing and the fork moves the pivot arm which in turn moves the hands.

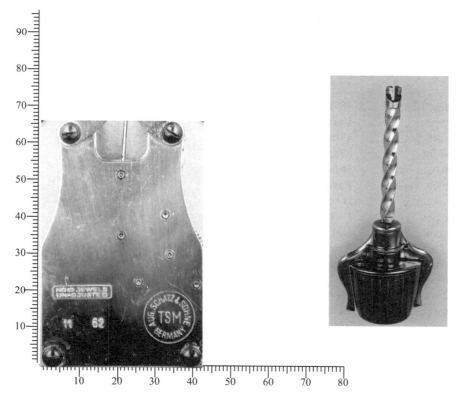

Schatz miniature TSM
43 x 67 x 10mm

Notes
The pendulum has a permanent magnet in its base. As the magnet passes over the outer 'Trigger' coil it induces a current at the base of the transistor. This current turns the PNP transistor on momentarily, allowing current to pass through the transistor, energising the centrally located repulse coil. The repulse coil gives the magnet an electromagnetic 'push' or repulse. The capacitor across this coil is also charged by the momentary current from the transistor. It acts as a small reservoir of energy which increases the duration of the push while it discharges.

Rapid Recognition Tips
Electromagnetic aperture in base

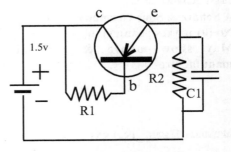

R1 Outer trigger coil 0.66k ohms
R2 Inner repulse coil 1.88k ohms
C1 10uF electrolytic

Data
Movement ID Code ...... **JS-TSM**
Plate shape .... **Vest**
Plate width **43mm**
Plate height **67mm**
Gap between plates **10mm**
Escapement type .... **Pawl**
Battery voltage .... **D cell 1.5v**
Repulse coil .... **1,880 ohms**
Trigger coil .... **660 ohms**
Locking device: .... **None**
Pendulum type/s .... **1-ball lateral**
Mainspring barrel .... **n/s**
Transistor .... **Germanium PNP**
Capacitor .... **10uF electrolytic**
Suspension .... **n/a**
Mainspring .... **n/a**
Beats per minute ....
Bob weight .... **70g.**

Examples of clocks fitted with the Schatz TSM Electromagnetic movement

Manufacturer:
Jahresuhrenfabrik
A. Schatz & Söhne

Backplate information:
A Schatz & Sons Germany 59
No (0) JEWELS UNADJUSTED
**May show month & year of
manufacture**

Model:
Schatz Balance Wheel 59
8 Day
64mm x 101mm x 20mm

Movement ID code: **JS-59**

Notes:
Although only an 8-Day clock, this was still in the style of an Anniversary Clock.

Schatz 8 day 59
curved legs
64x 101 x 20mm (including legs)

Notes

The support legs for this movement and the plates are combined into one piece.

The slow 1-second-per-beat balance wheel gives an illusion of a clock going for more than 8 days.

Domed models have a plastic dome with brass lugs that twists into place.

Rapid Recognition Tips

The only movement marked with Schatz 59. Distinctive balance wheel

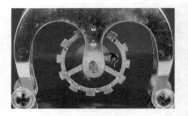

Data

Movement ID Code	**JS-59**
Plate shape	**Legged, curved**
Plate width	**64mm**
Plate height	**101mm**
Gap between plates	**20mm**
Escapement type	**Pin pallet**
Original key size	**Threaded winder**
Winding side	**Central**
Pivot adjuster	**n/a**
Locking device:	**None**
Pendulum type/s	**Balance wheel**
Mainspring barrel	**35mm x 14mm**
Replacement wire	**n/a**
Replacement unit	**n/a**
Jig settings	**n/a**
Mainspring	**n/a**
Beats per minute	**60**
Bob weight	**n/a**

Examples of clocks fitted with the Schatz 59 Balance wheel movement

 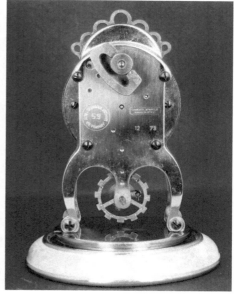

J. Kaiser GmbH

Kaiser Clocks became famous due to their distinctive Globe pendulums, and as such, are very easy to identify.

Kaiser also made Standard 4-ball clocks, but not all the movements stamped with their name were made by them.

In particular, their 67mm x 89mm Standard movement was manufactured by W. Petersen. The serrated nuts holding the back-plate and the unusual fork are immediately recognizable as Petersen characteristics. This movement is covered in the W. Petersen section.

A typical Kaiser globe

The Kaiser mark on a Petersen movement.

Kaiser listings:

Manufacturer:
J. Kaiser GmbH

Model:
Kaiser Standard narrow 'Universe'
44mm x 88mm x 30mm

Backplate information:
May have
J. Kaiser GmbH
Villingen
Germany
No (0) jewels
Unadjusted
Foreign

Movement ID code: **JK-SN**

Notes:
The visible pendulum is a hollow globe mounted on the suspension. The real pendulum is beneath the base. The lunar globe at the top rotates once every 30 days.

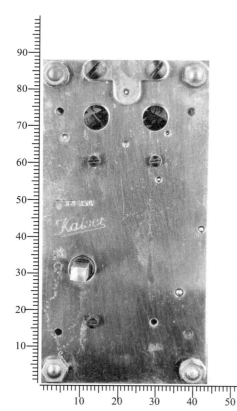

The real pendulum is inside the base

Kaiser Universe
44 x 88 x 30mm

Notes

Although initially named the 'Universe', the name had to be withdrawn as it was already a registered trademark. It was later known as the 'World Timepiece'.

The bob consists of four weights. Two are fixed and two are moved in and out by pins that locate in the eccentric disc under the base.

Rapid Recognition Tips

Unmistakeable Globe pendulum.

Data

Movement ID Code	**JK-SN**
Plate shape	**Rectangular**
Plate width	**44mm**
Plate height	**88mm**
Gap between plates	**30mm**
Escapement type	**Dead beat**
Original key size	**4.00mm**
Winding side	**Left**
Pivot adjuster	**Screwed bracket**
Locking device:	**Beneath the base**
Pendulum type/s	**Globe**
Mainspring barrel	**22.8mm x 44mm**
Replacement wire	**No. 10 (Horolovar™ 0.003"/0.076mm)**
Replacement unit	**JK-SN (Horolovar™ 34)**
Jig settings	**98mm, 103mm**
Mainspring	**19 x 0.40 x 38mm (1350mm)**
Beats per minute	**8**
Bob weight	**250g.**

Examples of clocks fitted with the Kaiser Standard narrow movement

Kern & Söhne

Kern & Söhne produced a wide range of post war Anniversary clock
Identifying that a clock was made by Kern is, unfortunately, far easi
than identifying exactly which one it is. The three exceptions to this a
the K.u.S.-PI, K.u.S-MIV and the K.u.S.-SIV. They are not alwa
marked with these codes.

For the remaining models, especially the 44mm x 60mm plate size,
you need to compare the back plate with the images on the relevant
pages.

Kern & Söhne succeeded Kern & Link who had acquired Kienzle
Clock Factories.

J Link opened his own factory many years later.

The three very easy models to identify

Kern & Söhne listings:

KS logos.

By model:

By Movement Identity Code:

By dimensions:

Rectangular

*Kern movements do not use traditional click springs;
they normally use coiled springs with one end coiled
around one of the pillars on the movement.*

Manufacturer:
Kern & Söhne

Model:
Kern Standard early
69mm x 93mm x 30mm

Backplate information:
May have:
KS in a dashed double circle, with or
without Germany

Movement ID code: **KS-SE**

Notes:
This is the original full width standard model based on the original Kern & Link design. There are two version. This is the earlier version with no pendulum locking. Not to be confused with the later version that had two bracket screw holes at the bottom of the back plate.

No Bracket screw holes at the
bottom of the back plate.

Kern Standard early
69 x 93 x 30mm

Notes
As this movement had no locking bracket, there should be no pendulum cup in the base.

Movements looking very similar to this can be found but closer inspection may show that they were assembled by Kern from parts they acquired when they purchased Schlenker & Posner in the late 1930's. Refer to the Schlenker & Posner section if there are inspection holes in the front plate even if stamped with the Kern logo.

Rapid Recognition Tips
Look for the curved cut-out in the platform, to make room for the suspension wire and guard.

Data
Movement ID Code	**KS-SE**
Plate shape	**Rectangular**
Plate width	**69mm**
Plate height	**93mm**
Gap between plates	**30mm**
Escapement type	**Dead beat**
Original key size	**4.50mm**
Winding side	**Left**
Pivot adjuster	**Eccentric nut**
Locking device:	**None**
Pendulum type/s	**4-ball**
Mainspring barrel	**21mm x 42mm**
Replacement wire	**No. 16 (Horolovar™ 0.0036"/0.091mm)**
Replacement unit	**KS-SE (Horolovar™ 11A)**
Jig settings	**110mm, 118mm**
Mainspring	**18 x 0.45 x 38mm (1120mm)**
Beats per minute	**8**
Bob weight	**280g.**

Examples of clocks fitted with the Kern & Link/Kern Standard early movement.

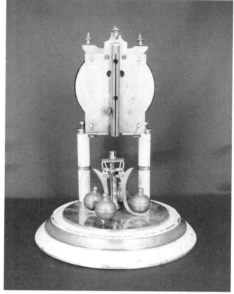

Manufacturer:
Kern & Söhne

Model:
Kern Standard late
69mm x 93mm x 30mm

Backplate information:
May have:
KS in a dashed double circle
Germany

Movement ID code: **KS-SL**

Notes:
This is the original full width standard model. This is the later version with pendulum locking that uses a bracket screwed to the bottom of the backplate.
Not to be confused with the earlier version that had no bracket holes at the bottom.

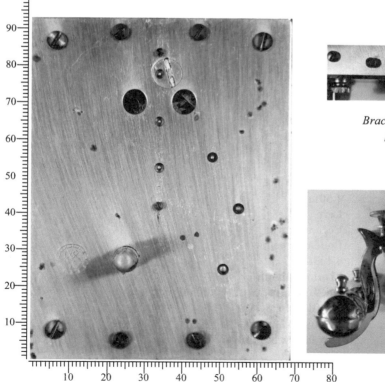

Bracket screw
holes

Kern Standard late
69 x 93 x 30mm

Notes
As this later movement had a locking bracket,
there should be a pendulum cup in the base

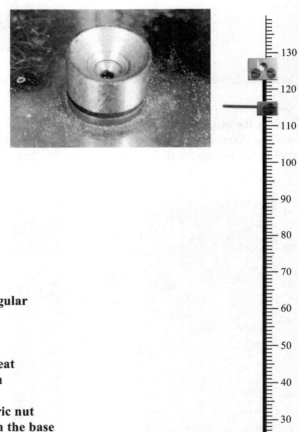

Rapid Recognition Tips

Data
Movement ID Code ...... **KS-SL**
Plate shape .... **Rectangular**
Plate width **69mm**
Plate height **93mm**
Gap between plates **30mm**
Escapement type .... **Dead beat**
Original key size **4.50mm**
Winding side .... **Left**
Pivot adjuster .... **Eccentric nut**
Locking device: .... **Beneath the base**
Pendulum type/s **4-ball**
Mainspring barrel .... **21mm x 42mm**
Replacement wire .... **No. 16 (Horolovar™ 0.0036"/0.091mm)**
Replacement unit .... **KS-SL (Horolovar™ 11B)**
Jig settings **115mm, 123mm**
Mainspring .... **18 x 0.45 x 38mm (1120mm)**
Beats per minute **8**
Bob weight .... **280g.**

Examples of clocks fitted with the Kern Standard late movement.

 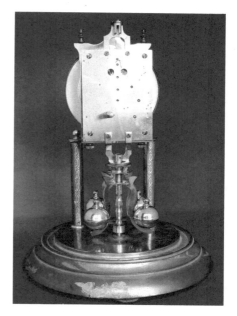

Manufacturer:
Kern & Söhne

Model:
Kern Standard narrow (SIV)
44mm x 93mm x 30mm

Backplate information:
May have:
KS in a dashed circle
No (0) JEWELS UNADJUSTED
KERN & SÖHNE GERMANY
K.u.S.-SIV

Movement ID code: **KS-SN**

Notes:
This is the narrow version of the earlier standard model. The standard train was rearranged into a narrower plate. Frequently found marked with just K.u.S. SIV

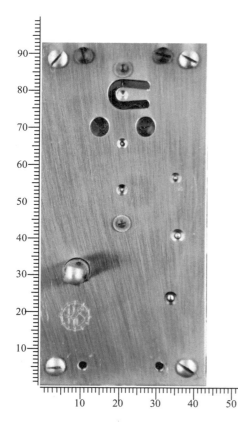

Kern Standard narrow
44 x 93 x 30mm

Notes
Most of the parts in the Standard Narrow movement are identical to the wider Standard movement with the exception of the plates.

Rapid Recognition Tips
Those marked K.u.S.-SIV are immediately identifiable.

Data

Movement ID Code	**KS-SN**
Plate shape	**Rectangular**
Plate width	**44mm**
Plate height	**93mm**
Gap between plates	**30mm**
Escapement type..........	**Dead beat**
Original key size	**4.50mm**
Winding side	**Left**
Pivot adjuster...............	**Adjustable arm**
Locking device:	**Beneath the base**
Pendulum type/s	**4-ball**
Mainspring barrel	**21mm x 42mm**
Replacement wire	**No. 16 (Horolovar™ 0.0036"/0.091mm)**
Replacement unit..........	**KS-SL (Horolovar™ 11B)**
Jig settings	**116mm, 123mm**
Mainspring	**18 x 0.45 x 38mm (1120mm)**
Beats per minute...........	**8**
Bob weight	**280g.**

Examples of clocks fitted with the Kern Standard narrow movement.

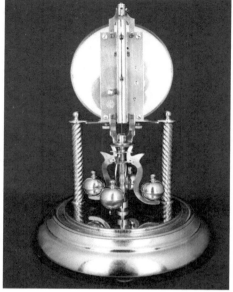

Manufacturer:
Kern & Söhne

Backplate information:
May have:
KS in a dashed circle
KERN & SÖHNE GERMANY
NO (0) JEWELS UNADJUSTED

Model:
Kern Miniature
Lefthand winder, Eccentric nut
44mm x 60mm x 20mm

Movement ID code: **KS-MLE**

Notes:
This model has the winder on the left. Two variations of this model exist. This one has the eccentric nut. Not to be confused with the model that uses a screwed bracket adjuster, although the plate dimensions and wheels appear identical.

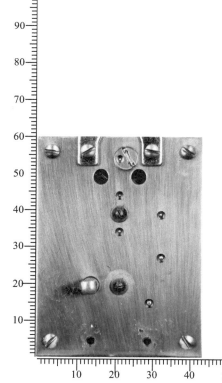

Eccentric nut adjuster

Kern Miniature
Lefthand winder, Eccentric nut
44 x 60 x 20mm

Notes
Publisher's note:
The author is aware that a small number of clocks using this movement use a slightly shorter, thinner wire, but has yet to establish exactly how to identify which clock cases are affected in this way. It appears to affect cases that restrict the width of the pendulum and the contents of the balls may vary.

Rapid Recognition Tips

Data
Movement ID Code ...... **KS-MLE**
Plate shape .... **Rectangular**
Plate width **44mm**
Plate height **60mm**
Gap between plates **20mm**
Escapement type .... **Dead beat**
Original key size **3.50mm**
Winding side .... **Left**
Pivot adjuster .... **Eccentric nut**
Locking device: .... **Beneath the base**
Pendulum type/s **4-ball**
Mainspring barrel .... **14mm x 27mm**
Replacement wire .... **No. 3 (Horolovar™ 0.0020"/0.051mm)**
Replacement unit .... **KS-ML (Horolovar™ 12C)**
Jig settings **73mm, 77mm**
Mainspring .... **12 x 0.35 x 25mm (700mm)**
Beats per minute **6**
Bob weight .... **255g.**

Examples of clocks fitted with the KS Miniature lefthand eccentric nut movement

Manufacturer:
Kern & Söhne

Model:
Kern Miniature
Lefthand wind, bracket
44mm x 60mm x 20mm

Backplate information:
May have:
KS in a dashed double circle
KERN U. SÖHNE GERMANY
NO (0) JEWELS UNADJUSTED

Movement ID code: **KS-MLB**

Notes:
This model has the winder on the left. Two variations of this model exist. This one has the screwed bracket adjuster. Not to be confused with the model that uses an eccentric nut, although the plate dimensions and wheels appear identical.

Screwed bracket adjuster

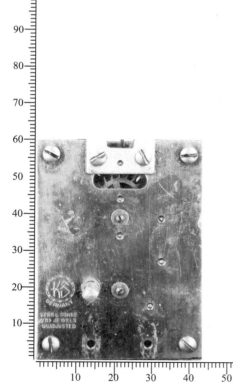

Kern Miniature
Lefthand winder, bracket
44 x 60 x 20mm

Notes

Publisher's note:

The author is aware that a small number of clocks using this movement use a slightly shorter, thinner wire, but has yet to establish exactly how to identify which clock cases are affected in this way. It appears to affect cases that restrict the width of the pendulum and the contents of the balls may vary.

Rapid Recognition Tips

Data

Movement ID Code	**KS-MLB**
Plate shape	**Rectangular**
Plate width	**44mm**
Plate height	**60mm**
Gap between plates	**20mm**
Escapement type	**Dead beat**
Original key size	**3.50mm**
Winding side	**Left**
Pivot adjuster	**Screwed bracket**
Locking device:	**Beneath the base**
Pendulum type/s	**4-ball**
Mainspring barrel	**14mm x 27mm**
Replacement wire	**No. 3 (Horolovar™ 0.0020"/0.051mm)**
Replacement unit	**KS-ML (Horolovar™ 12C)**
Jig settings	**73mm, 77mm**
Mainspring	**12 x 0.35x 25mm (700mm)**
Beats per minute	**6**
Bob weight	**255g.**

Examples of clocks fitted with the KS Miniature lefthand screwed bracket movement

Manufacturer:
Kern & Söhne

Backplate information:
May have:
KS in a dashed circle
KERN & SÖHNE GERMANY
NO (0) JEWELS UNADJUSTED
OR
K.U.S. MIV

Movement ID code: **KS-MINR**

Notes:
This model has the winder on the right, and is frequently found in lantern cases, either rectangular or triangular with plastic sides.

Either marked KS or K.u.S. MIV but not both

Model:
Kern Miniature (MIV)
Right-hand side winder
44mm x 60mm x 21mm

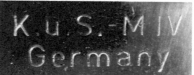

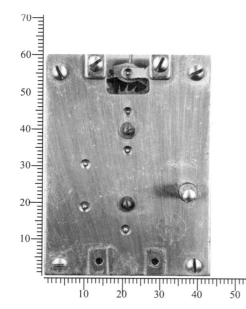

Kern Miniature (MIV)
Right-hand side winder
44 x 60 x 21mm

Notes
Many consider the movement marked KS to be a different to the movement marked K.u.S MIV.

The problem appears to be due to a discrepancy in the mainsprings fitted. It is common to find a shorter, weaker spring in a K.u.S MIV movement but the barrels are identical and there is room for the spring shown below.

Rapid Recognition Tips
The only model with the KS logo on the backplate and the winding shaft on the right. Those bearing the K.u.S. MIV stamp are instantly recognizable.

Data
Movement ID Code ...... **KS-MINR**
Plate shape .... **Rectangular**
Plate width **44mm**
Plate height **60mm**
Gap between plates **21mm**
Escapement type .... **Dead beat**
Original key size **3.50mm**
Winding side .... **Right**
Pivot adjuster.............. **Adjustable arm**
Locking device: .... **Beneath the base**
Pendulum type/s **4-ball**
Mainspring barrel .... **17mm x 33mm**
Replacement wire .... **No. 6 (Horolovar™ 0.0023"/0.058mm)**
Replacement unit .... **KS-MR (Horolovar™ 12F)**
Jig settings **73mm, 77mm**
Mainspring .... **14 x 0.35 x 30mm (815mm)**
Beats per minute **8**
Bob weight .... **255g.**

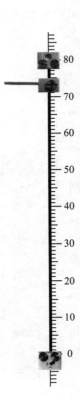

Examples of clocks fitted with the KS Miniature right-hand wind movement

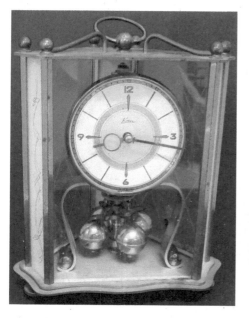 

Manufacturer:
Kern & Söhne

Model:
Kern Miniature Remontoire
44mm x 60mm x 20mm

Backplate information:
May have:
KS in a dashed circle

Movement ID code: **KS-REM**

Notes:
Although technically a battery movement, the battery only applies a pulse every 4 minutes to maintain mechanical power to the train. It is in fact weight driven, as a small weight on an arm is lifted at each impulse.

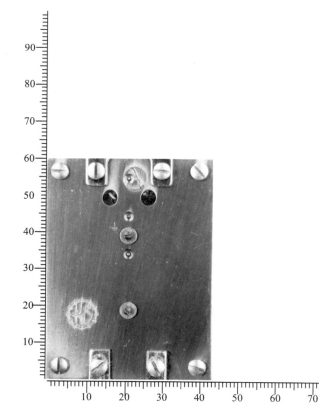

Kern Miniature Remontoire
44 x 60 x 20mm

The weight attached to an arm.

Notes
When the weight on an arm drops below a fixed point, a pair of electrical contacts make contact. This powers the solenoid which kicks the arm bearing the weight back up. The battery is mounted beneath the base. 3v penlight 2R10 batteries are still available but can be hard to find, Two AA batteries in a suitable holder taped to the base will operate the clock.

When you change the battery, take a cotton bud dipped in alcohol and clean the electrical contacts.

Rapid Recognition Tips
KS with no winding shaft on the backplate.

Visible solenoid mechanism.

Solenoid

Data

Movement ID Code	**KS-REM**
Plate shape	**Rectangular**
Plate width	**44mm**
Plate height	**60mm**
Gap between plates	**20mm**
Escapement type	**Dead beat**
Battery	**Penlight 3v 2R10**
Winding side	**n/a**
Pivot adjuster	**Eccentric nut**
Locking device:	**Beneath the base**
Pendulum type/s	**4-ball**
Mainspring barrel	**n/a**
Replacement wire	**No. 2 (Horolovar™ 0.0019"/0.048mm)**
Replacement unit	**KS-MLT (Horolovar™ 12D)**
Jig settings	**72mm, 76mm**
Mainspring	**n/a**
Beats per minute	**6**
Bob weight	**255g.**

Examples of clocks fitted with the KS miniature remontoire movement

Manufacturer:
Kern & Söhne

Model:
Kern Midget (K.u.S. PI)
44mm x 54mm x 21mm

Backplate information:
KS Logo
May have Kerne & Söhne, Germany.
May have No (0) jewels, Unadjusted.
K.u.S. PI
Tubular wire guard and clip-on top guard.

Movement ID code: **KS-MIDG**

Notes:
This movement has its pallet arbor pivot hole in a delicate arm that can be adjusted by bending. Marked either KS or K.u.S.PI.
K.u.S. stood for <u>K</u>ern <u>u</u>nd (&) <u>S</u>öhne.

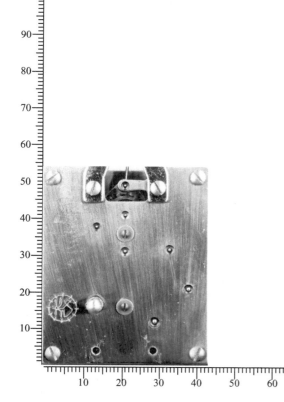

Kern Midget (K.u.S. PI)
44 x 54 x 21mm

Tubular suspension guard

Notes
The Kern Midget was made in large numbers in the 1950's.

Fork guard

Rapid Recognition Tips
A movement of 44mm x 54mm stamped with the KS logo is a Kern Midget.
K.u.S.PI is a unique mark that applies to this movement, but not all movements have this stamped on them.

Data
Movement ID Code	**KS-MIDG**
Plate shape	**Rectangular**
Plate width	**44mm**
Plate height	**54mm**
Gap between plates	**21mm**
Escapement type	**Pin pallet**
Original key size	**3.75mm**
Winding side	**Left**
Pivot adjuster	**Adjustable arm**
Locking device:	**Beneath the base**
Pendulum type/s	**4-ball**
Mainspring barrel	**16mm x 28mm**
Replacement wire	**No. 6 (Horolovar™ 0.0023"/0.058mm)**
Replacement unit	**KS-MD (Horolovar™ 12E)**
Jig settings	**67mm, 71mm**
Mainspring	**14 x 0.35 x 25mm (700mm)**
Beats per minute	**12**
Bob weight	**134g.**

Examples of clocks fitted with the Kern Midget movement

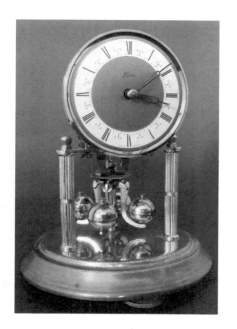

Examples of clocks fitted with the Kern

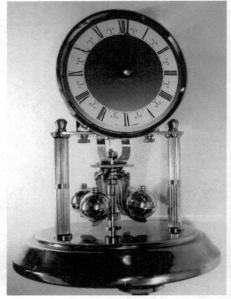

Kieninger & Obergfell

Kieninger & Obergfell produced Anniversary Clocks in vast numbers, especially in the post war years, using the brand name of Kundo, derived from K und (&) O. Earlier clocks were often stamped with the somewhat confusing KO logo.

Despite the vast numbers produced, the range of movements is very small, and this can be put down to their design success, particularly in the latter years.

The rather confusing KO logo.

The later markings.

The Kundo locking device, used on all later torsion movements, is an immediate way to identify the manufacturer.

Kieninger & Obergfell listings:

By dimensions:

Manufacturer:

Kieninger & Obergfell

Model:

K&O Standard movement, eccentric

Backplate information:

May have:
KO Logo
Kieninger & Obergfell
Made in Germany

Normally has the rather confusing KO logo in script within a circle

Movement ID code: **KO-SE**

Notes:

This early model has an eccentric nut adjuster, and the plates are 2mm wider than the later standard model.

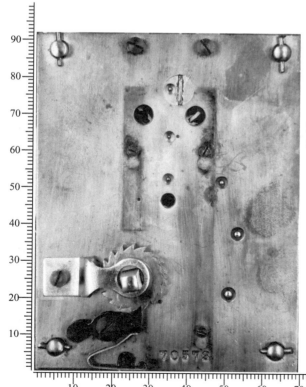

This movement has an eccentric nut to adjust the pivot position.

K&O Standard movement, eccentric
70 x 92 x 30mm

Notes

Early locking devices were primitive, and provided very little protection.

First type of locking guard

The guard was a square tube screwed to the back plate. The locking devices slid down inside the tube, to secure the bottom block and the hook.

Second type of locking guard

Rapid Recognition Tips

Data

Movement ID Code	**KO-SE**
Plate shape	**Rectangular**
Plate width	**70mm**
Plate height	**92mm**
Gap between plates	**30mm**
Escapement type	**Dead beat**
Original key size	**4.50mm**
Winding side	**Left**
Pivot adjuster	**Eccentric nut**
Locking device:	**On the guard**
Pendulum type/s	**4-ball**
Mainspring barrel	**22mm x 42mm**
Replacement wire	**No. 12 (Horolovar™ 0.0032"/0.081mm)**
Replacement unit	**KO-S (Horolovar™ 1)**
Jig settings	**106mm, 116mm**
Mainspring	**19 x 0.40 x 38mm (1350mm)**
Beats per minute	**8**
Bob weight	**240g.**

130
110
100
90
80
70
60
50
40
30
20
10
0

Examples of clocks fitted with the Kieninger & Obergfell eccentric movement

Manufacturer:
Kieninger & Obergfell

Model:
K&O Standard, arm adjuster
68mm x 92mm x 30mm

Backplate information:
May have:
KO Logo
Kieninger & Obergfell
Made in Germany

Normally has the rather confusing KO logo in script within a circle

Movement ID code: **KO-SA**

Notes:
This later model has an arm that could be bent to adjust the pivot position, and the plates are 2mm narrower than the earlier standard model.

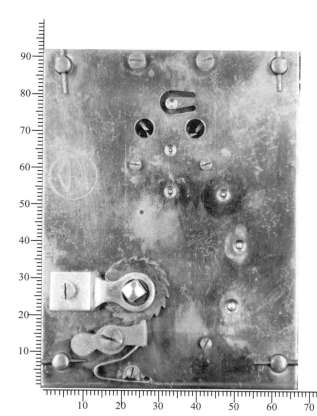

This movement has an arm to adjust the pivot position.

K&O Standard movement, arm adjuster
68 x 92 x 30mm

Notes

Early locking devices were primitive, and provided very little protection. The final version of this model had a ring type locking device that required a special bottom block.

Standard locking guard

The guard was a square tube screwed to the back plate. Both types of locking devices slid down inside the tube, to secure the bottom block.

Rapid Recognition Tips

A plate of 66mm x 92mm with a horizontal arm adjuster identifies this movement.

The later 'ring' type guard

Data

Movement ID Code	**KO-SA**
Plate shape	**Rectangular**
Plate width	**68mm**
Plate height	**92mm**
Gap between plates	**30mm**
Escapement type	**Dead beat**
Original key size	**4.50mm**
Winding side	**Left**
Pivot adjuster	**Adjustable arm**
Locking device:	**On the guard**
Pendulum type/s	**4-ball**
Mainspring barrel	**22mm x 42mm**
Replacement wire	**No. 12 (Horolovar™ 0.0032"/0.081mm)**
Replacement unit	**KO-S (Horolovar™ 1)**
Jig settings	**106mm, 116mm**
Mainspring	**19 x 0.40 x 38mm (1350mm)**
Beats per minute	**8**
Bob weight	**222g.**

Examples of clocks fitted with the Kieninger & Obergfell standard arm movement

Manufacturer:
Kieninger & Obergfell

Model:
K&O Standard narrow
44mm x 93mm x 30mm

Backplate information:
May have:
KO Logo
Kieninger & Obergfell
Made in West Germany
No (0) jewels, Unadjusted.

Movement ID code: **KO-SN**

Notes:
Early models had screwed suspension guards. Later models had plastic guards that snapped into D shaped holes.

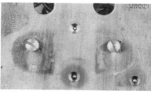

Screw holes for the earlier suspension guard.

'D' shaped holes for the later plastic suspension guard.

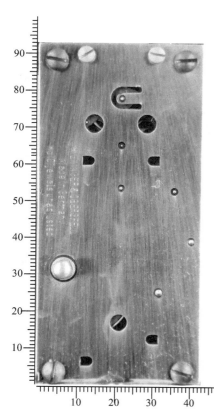

The earlier plate with three screws on the guard (1/2 size)

K&O Standard narrow movement
44 x 93 x 30mm

Lever locking pin

Notes

The locking mechanism changed during production. Very early models had a fixed pin the bottom block, but were soon replaced with split pins and finally loose pins held in by a shaped washer.

Replacement units are normally supplied with fixed pins. You will have to push out the fixed pin and enlarge the hole to reuse the loose pin.

To prevent the locking lever moving during shipping, a split pin was inserted vertically through the hole on the left of the platform.

Rapid Recognition Tips

Only this movement has plates 44mm x 93mm and a locking device on the platform as illustrated.

Models with the D shaped guard holes are immediately identifiable.

The Kundo locking device, used from this movement onwards.

Data

Movement ID Code ...... **KO-SN**
Plate shape .... **Rectangular**
Plate width **44mm**
Plate height **93mm**
Gap between plates **30mm**
Escapement type .... **Dead beat**
Original key size **4.50mm**
Winding side .... **Left**
Pivot adjuster .... **Adjustable arm**
Locking device: .... **On the platform**
Pendulum type/s **4-ball**
Mainspring barrel .... **23mm x 42mm**
Replacement wire .... **No. 12 (Horolovar™ 0.0032"/0.081mm)**
Replacement unit .... **KO-SN (Horolovar™ 3C)**
Jig settings **106mm, 116mm**
Mainspring .... **19 x 0.40 x 38mm (1350mm)**
Beats per minute **8**
Bob weight .... **218g.**

Examples of clocks fitted with the Kieninger & Obergfell narrow movement

Manufacturer:
Kieninger & Obergfell

Model:
K&O Miniature
44mm x 70mm x 23mm

Backplate information:
May have:
Kundo
Kieninger & Obergfell
Made in West Germany
No (0) jewels, Unadjusted.

The early and somewhat confusing KO logo.

The later Kundo logo.

Movement ID code: **KO-MIN**

Notes:
Not to be confused with the midget movement that had the same plate size but had a rectangular cutout at the bottom. If the suspension guard has two upper screws (or if missing, screw holes), it is an early model.

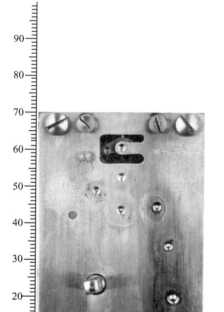

Early guard with two upper screws

Later guard with one upper screw

Two types of bob were fitted. Both use the same suspension wire.

K&O Miniature
44 x 70 x 23mm

Notes
The locking mechanism on miniature movements changed during production. Very early models had a fixed pin holding the bob in place, but these were soon replaced with split pins and finally loose pins held in by a shaped washer as the design of the locking mechanism evolved.

Replacement units are normally supplied with fixed pins. You will have to push out the pin and enlarge the hole to reuse the loose pin.

Rapid Recognition Tips
Only this movement has plates 44mm x 70mm with no cutout at the bottom and a locking device on the platform as illustrated.

The platform that supports the movement is normally 75mm above the base.

To prevent the locking lever moving during shipping, a split pin was inserted vertically through the hole on the left of the platform.

The Kundo locking device, used on all miniature and midget movements

Data
Movement ID Code	**KO-MIN**
Plate shape	**Rectangular**
Plate width	**44mm**
Plate height	**70mm**
Gap between plates	**23mm**
Escapement type	**Dead beat**
Original key size	**3.50mm**
Winding side	**Left**
Pivot adjuster	**Adjustable arm**
Locking device:	**Under the platform**
Pendulum type/s	**4-ball**
Mainspring barrel	**17mm x 34mm**
Replacement wire	**No. 6 (Horolovar™ 0.0023"/0.058mm)**
Replacement unit	**KO-MIN (Horolovar™ 5E)**
Jig settings	**80mm, 83mm**
Mainspring	**14 x 0.35 x 30mm (815mm)**
Beats per minute	**10**
Bob weight	**158g.**

Examples of clocks fitted with the Kieninger & Obergfell miniature movement

The Kundo with a Miniature movement was fitted with a re-designed bob that reduced the height without modification to the movement.

The Miniature movement in what was the smallest style of its kind ever produced.

Manufacturer:
Kieninger & Obergfell

Model:
K&O Midget
44mm x 70mm x 23mm

Backplate information:
May have:
Kundo
Kieninger & Obergfell
Made in West Germany
No (0) jewels, Unadjusted.

Movement ID code: **KO-MIDG**

Notes:
The Kundo Midget movement is ironically the same size as the miniature movement, but has a distinctive rectangular cutout at the base. This was to prevent the pendulum hook assembly from touching the plate.

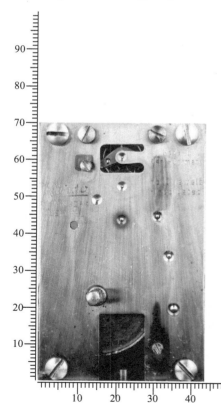

The pendulum hook arrangement was raised above the platform.

K&O Midget
44 x 70 x 23mm

Notes
To create a midget using a miniature movement involved creating a very short pendulum and using a shorter suspension. The plate had a rectangle cut out at the base to make room for the high pendulum hook and its locking washers.

To prevent the locking lever moving during shipping a split pin was inserted vertically through the hole on the left of the platform.

The high pendulum hook required a cutout in the backplate

Replacement units are normally supplied with fixed pins. You will have to push out the pin and enlarge the hole to reuse the loose pin

Rapid Recognition Tips
The only Kieninger & Obergfell/Kundo backplate with a rectangle cut out at the base. The pendulum hook is above the platform. The platform that supports the movement is normally only 40mm above the base.

Data
Movement ID Code	**KO-MIDG**
Plate shape	**Rectangular**
Plate width	**44mm**
Plate height	**70mm**
Gap between plates	**23mm**
Escapement type	**Dead beat**
Original key size	**3.50mm**
Winding side	**Left**
Pivot adjuster	**Adjustable arm**
Locking device:	**Under the platform**
Pendulum type/s	**4-ball**
Mainspring barrel	**17mm x 34mm**
Replacement wire	**No. 5 (Horolovar™ 0.0022"/0.056mm)**
Replacement unit	**KO-MID (Horolovar™ 5F)**
Jig settings	**58mm, 62mm**
Mainspring	**14 x 0.35 x 30mm (815mm)**
Beats per minute	**10**
Bob weight	**144g.**

Examples of clocks fitted with the Kieninger & Obergfell midget movement

 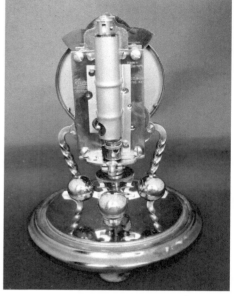

Manufacturer:
Kieninger & Obergfell

Model:
K&O Electronic (ATO)
36mm Round

Backplate information:
A plain unmarked circular plate with 6 jewels.

The swing of the pendulum drives the clock by a pawl attached to the pendulum hook.

Movement ID code: **KO-ATO**

Notes:
This ATO type clock used a small circuit board under the base of early models to drive an electromagnetic coil to swing the pendulum. Later models had the circuitry inside the coil housing. It is not easy to recognize if a coil needs a separate circuit board as these were glued under the base. If it has come away, there may be glue marks. The early ones (with and without a PCB) used a large flat battery but final models used a plastic D cell holder.

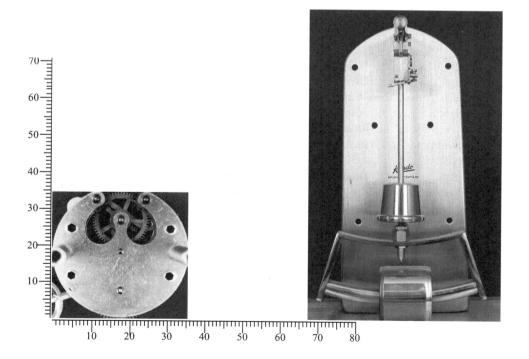

14-24 Kieninger

K&O Electronic (ATO)
36 mm diameter x 8mm

The suspension is similar to a mantel clock.

The early coil needing a PCB.

Notes
ATO was originally a brand, named after Leon Hâtot who first produced a transistorized pendulum clock, but the term ATO has spread to cover most examples.

As the magnet at one end of the pendulum passes through the coil, it induces a current which triggers the energisation of the coil, causing an electromagnetic 'push' of the pendulum.

The germanium transistors used on the circuit board have a limited life due to the growth of whiskers inside the can. It is not possible to replace them with silicone transistors.

The later coil needing no PCB.

Rapid Recognition Tips
Distinctive arc pendulum moving through a coil

Data

Movement ID Code	**KO-ATO**
Plate shape	**Circular**
Plate width	**36mm**
Plate height	**36mm**
Gap between plates	**8mm**
Escapement type	**Pawl**
Voltage	**1.5v**
Battery	**D cell or flat 1.5v,** AA Adapters are available.
Pivot adjuster	**n/a**
Locking device:	**Rear screw**
Pendulum type/s	**Lateral**
Mainspring barrel	**n/a**
Replacement wire	**n/a**
Replacement unit	**17mm wide, 16mm high.**
Jig settings	**n/a**
Mainspring	**n/a**
Beats per minute	**42**
Bob weight	**140g.**

PCB

17mm wide
16mm high

Examples of clocks fitted with the Kieninger & Obergfell ATO style movement

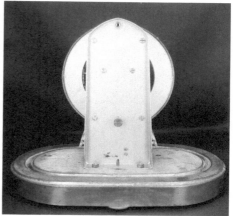

Kienzle Clock Factories

Kienzle Clock Factories, later to become Kern & Link, were one of the earlier manufacturers, but care must be taken not to assume that a clock with Kienzle on the dial has a movement that was made by them.

If the movement has lantern pinon and not pinions cut from solid steel, it was probably bought by them from Andreas Huber, who also supplied Badische Uhrenfabrik.These are more common than a conventional Kienzle example.

The lantern pinion movements have been described in the past as having been made by Badische Uhrenfabrik, but this now seems highly unlikely.

Lantern pinions are made with wires and not cut from solid steel. If the movement has lantern pinions, refer to the Badische Uhrenfabrik pages. Badische Uhrenfabrik were the main users of these lantern movements.

The Kienzle Clock Factories logo can appear on the dial, but Badische/Huber movements were used widely in their 400 day clocks.

Kienzle listings:

By model:

By Movement Identity Code:

By dimensions:

Rectangular

Manufacturer:
Kienzle

Model:
Kienzle Standard
66mm x 88mm x 30mm

Backplate information:
May have:
KIENZLE CLOCK FACTORIES
SCHWENNINGEN
GERMANY
a Serial number

Movement ID code: **KC-STD**

The rings that guard the suspension, very often missing.

Notes:
The front escapement pivot is a replaceable bush, screwed in place.

The front escapement bush, screwed in place.

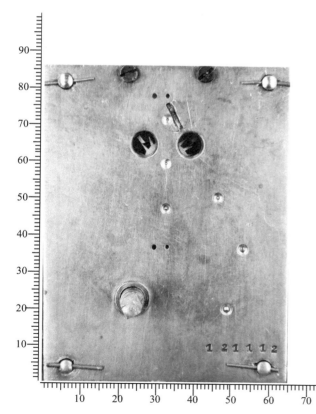

Kienzle Standard
66mm x 88mm x 30mm

Notes
The top block is normally an E shaped block in a bracket.

Internal ratchet.

Unlike the lantern pinion movements used on other clocks, these are more conventional 400 day movements.

Rapid Recognition Tips
The back-plate has two pairs of distinctive holes. Only the Gustav Becker Standard has a slightly similar feature, but that plate has an external ratchet.
Internal ratchet.

Data
Movement ID Code	**KC-STD**
Plate shape	**Rectangular**
Plate width	**66mm**
Plate height	**88mm**
Gap between plates	**30mm**
Escapement type	**Dead Beat**
Original key size	**4.25mm**
Winding side	**Left**
Pivot adjuster	**Eccentric nut**
Locking device:	**None**
Pendulum type/s	**Disc, 4-ball**
Mainspring barrel	**22mm x 42mm**
Replacement wire	**No. 16 (Horolovar™ 0.0036"/0.091mm)**
Replacement unit	**None, due to the top E-bracket.**
Jig settings	**102mm, 113mm**
Mainspring	**18 x 0.45 x 38mm (1120mm)**
Beats per minute	**8**
Bob weight	**270g.**

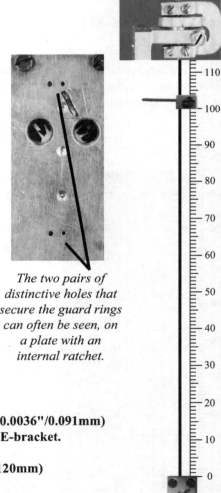

The two pairs of distinctive holes that secure the guard rings can often be seen, on a plate with an internal ratchet.

Examples of clocks fitted with the Kienzle Standard movement.

 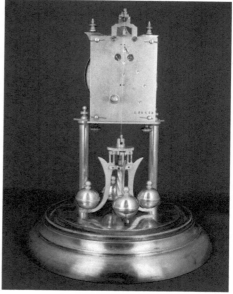

Konrad Mauch

Konrad Mauch started making clocks in 1921 and continued right up until the late 1950's.

As with a few other manufacturers, it is far easier to identify that a clock was made my Konrad Mauch than to identify which model it is.

The miniature and midget models had problems with the original strength of their mainsprings, and having identified a movement as being one of these two types, it is then necessary to identify if it has the weaker or stronger mainspring. Fortunately the suspension sizes did not change when the mainspring size was altered.

The distinctive cut out in the backplate of all but the very later models.

Konrad Mauch listings:

By model:

By Movement Identity Code:

By dimensions:

Manufacturer:
Konrad Mauch

Model:
Koma Standard Early
73mm x 85mm x 31mm

Backplate information:
**Koma beneath a semicircular
clock with the hands at 10:12**

Movement ID code: **KM-SE**

Notes:
This is the early model, with the conventional wide plates. The slightly later model had plates 7mm narrower than this model. The trains appear identical. The eccentric nut is on the frontplate.

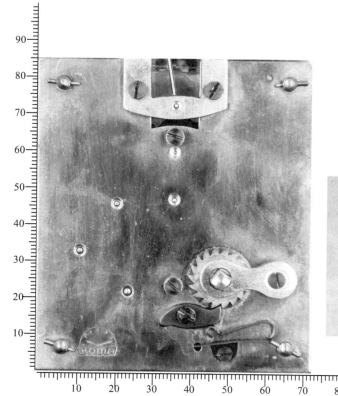

Koma Standard Early
73 x 85 x 31mm

Note the distinctive hinged flaps on the guard.

Notes

The eccentric nut is on the frontplate. The bracket on the backplate has no adjustment because it is too far from the pallets.

The square tube suspension guard incorporates two hinged side flaps that hold the bottom block in place. It is not intended to secure the pendulum.

Rapid Recognition Tips

The only movement 73mm wide with the Koma logo.

A standard sized movement with a winding shaft on the right is highly likely to have been made by Konrad Mauch.

The distinctive Koma cut-out in most back plates.

Data

Movement ID Code	**KM-SE**
Plate shape	**Rectangular**
Plate width	**73mm**
Plate height	**85mm**
Gap between plates	**31mm**
Escapement type	**Dead beat**
Original key size	**4.00mm**
Winding side	**Right**
Pivot adjuster	**Eccentric nut**
Locking device:	**On the guard**
Pendulum type/s	**4-ball**
Mainspring barrel	**23mm x40mm**
Replacement wire	**No. 15 (Horolovar™ 0.0035"/0.089mm)**
Replacement unit	**KM-S (Horolovar™ 13B)**
Jig settings	**115mm, 120mm**
Mainspring	**20 x 0.40 x 38mm (1350mm)**
Beats per minute	**8**
Bob weight	**285g.**

Examples of clocks fitted with the Konrad Mauch Standard early movement

Manufacturer:
Konrad Mauch

Model:
Koma Standard Late
66mm x 86mm x 31mm

Backplate information:
**Koma beneath a semicircular clock
with the hands at 10:12
Made in Germany**

Movement ID code: **KM-SL**

Notes:
This is the slightly later standard model, with plates 7mm narrower than the earlier wide plated standard model.

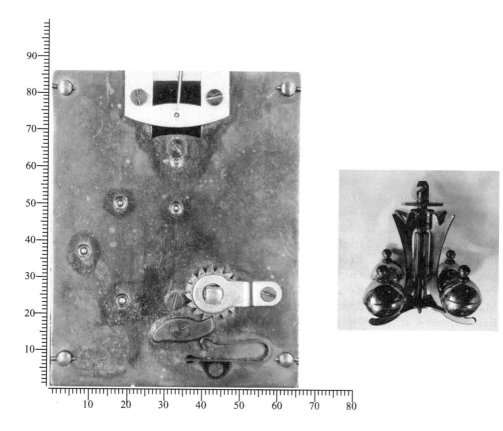

Koma Standard Late
66 x 86 x 31mm

Note the distinctive hinged flaps on the guard.

Notes

The eccentric nut is on the frontplate. The bracket on the backplate has no adjustment because it is too far from the pallets.

The square tube suspension guard incorporates two hinged side flaps that hold the bottom block in place. It is not intended to secure the pendulum.

The distinctive Koma cut-out in most back plates.

Rapid Recognition Tips

A standard sized movement with a winding shaft on the right is highly likely to be a Konrad Mauch.

Data

Movement ID Code	**KM-SL**
Plate shape	**Rectangular**
Plate width	**66mm**
Plate height	**86mm**
Gap between plates	**31mm**
Escapement type	**Dead beat**
Original key size	**4.00mm**
Winding side	**Right**
Pivot adjuster	**Eccentric nut**
Locking device:	**On the guard**
Pendulum type/s	**4-ball**
Mainspring barrel	**23mm x40mm**
Replacement wire	**No. 15 (Horolovar™ 0.0035"/0.089mm)**
Replacement unit	**KM-S (Horolovar™ 13B)**
Jig settings	**110mm, 115mm**
Mainspring	**20 x 0.40 x 38mm (1350mm)**
Beats per minute	**8**
Bob weight	**295g.**

Examples of clocks fitted with the Konrad Mauch Standard late movement

Manufacturer:
Konrad Mauch

Backplate information:
**Koma beneath a semicircular clock
with the hands at 10:12**

Model:
Kome Miniature early
External ratchet
42mm x 77mm x 25mm

Movement ID code: **KM-MINE**

Notes:
This is the early model, with the weaker mainspring. This proved too weak, and later models had a wider barrel, and two wheels rearranged to accommodate the change. The barrel on this model is 15.7mm wide. Not to be confused with the same size plate with the ratchet inside the front plate.

*This model has a 15.7mm mainspring barrel.
Note the larger gap between the barrel and the plate on this early model.*

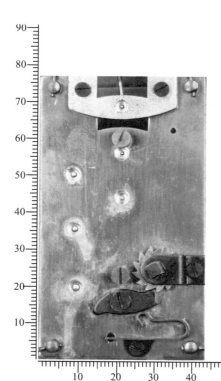

6mm (Wide) Gap

Koma miniature early
42 x 77 x 25mm

Notes
Lantern cased models may have screwed cases, so a rear hand setter was required. This is a shaft through the hole in the top right-hand corner of the plates, engaging with the motion work.

Early guard.   *Later guard.*

Early examples used the older style square suspension guard with flaps but this was later changed to a round tube.

Exception
Some movements were used with a 275g bob with 4 conical weights of solid brass. The additional weight and reduced diameter require a thinner wire. (Horolovar™ 0.076mm)

Rapid Recognition Tips

Solid brass bob needing a thinner wire.

Data

Movement ID Code	**KM-MINE**
Plate shape	**Rectangular**
Plate width	**42mm**
Plate height	**77mm**
Gap between plates	**25mm**
Escapement type	**Dead beat**
Original key size	**3.50mm**
Winding side	**Right**
Pivot adjuster	**Screwed bracket**
Locking device:	**Beneath the base**
Pendulum type/s	**4-ball**
Mainspring barrel	**15.7mm x 35mm**
Replacement wire	**No. 12 (Horolovar™ 0.0032"/0.081mm)**
Replacement unit	**KM-MIN (Horolovar™ 14A)**
Jig settings	**98mm, 103mm**
Mainspring	**13 x 0.55 x 32mm (715mm)**
Beats per minute	**8**
Bob weight	**232g.**

The distinctive Koma cut-out in most back plates.

— 130
— 120
— 110
— 100
— 90
— 80
— 70
— 60
— 50
— 40
— 30
— 20
— 10
— 0

Examples of clocks fitted with the Koma miniature early movement

The solid brass weights on this bob require a thinner wire due to the reduced diameter of the pendulum.

Manufacturer:
Konrad Mauch

Backplate information:
Koma beneath a semicircular clock
with hands at 10:12
Made in Germany

Model:
Koma miniature late,
external ratchet
42mm x 77mm x 25mm

Movement ID code: **KM-MINL**

External ratchet

Notes:
This is the later model, with the stronger mainspring. The spring on the earlier design proved too weak. This model had a wider barrel, with two wheels re-arranged to accommodate the change. Not to be confused with the same size plate with the ratchet inside the front plate.

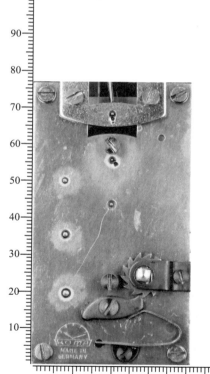

This model has a wider mainspring barrel. Note the reduced gap between the 18mm barrel and the plate on the late model.

4mm (Narrow) Gap

Koma miniature late, external ratchet
42 x 77 x 25mm

Notes

Lantern cased models may have screwed cases, so a rear hand setter was required. This is a shaft through the hole in the top right-hand corner of the plates, engaging with the motion work.

The hole for the lantern cased hand setter.

Rapid Recognition Tips

The distinctive Koma cut-out in most back plates.

Data

Movement ID Code	**KM-MINL**
Plate shape	**Rectangular**
Plate width	**42mm**
Plate height	**77mm**
Gap between plates	**25mm**
Escapement type	**Dead beat**
Original key size	**3.50mm**
Winding side	**Right**
Pivot adjuster	**Screwed bracket**
Locking device:	**On the guard**
Pendulum type/s	**4-ball**
Mainspring barrel	**18mm x 35mm**
Replacement wire	**No. 12 (Horolovar™ 0.0032"/0.081mm)**
Replacement unit	**KM-MIN (Horolovar™ 14A)**
Jig settings	**98mm, 103mm**
Mainspring	**15 x 0.50 x 32mm (760mm)**
Beats per minute	**8**
Bob weight	**232g.**

Examples of clocks fitted with the Koma miniature late external ratchet movement

Manufacturer:
Konrad Mauch

Backplate information:
**Koma beneath a semicircular clock
with hands at 10:12
Made in Germany**

Model:
Koma miniature late, internal ratchet
42mm x 77mm x 25mm

Internal ratchet, between the barrel and the front plate.

Movement ID code: **KM-MLI**

Notes:
This is the later model, with the stronger mainspring. The spring on the earlier design proved too weak. This model had a wider barrel, with two wheels re-arranged to accommodate the change. Not to be confused with the same size plate with the ratchet on the back plate.

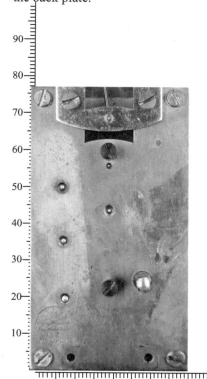

This model has a wider mainspring barrel. Note the reduced gap between the barrel and the plate.

Koma miniature late, internal ratchet
42 x 77 x 25mm

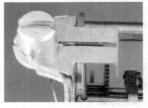

Notes
Lantern cased models may have screwed cases, so a rear hand setter was required. This is a shaft through the hole in the top right-hand corner of the plates, engaging with the motion work.

Later models were fitted with escapement guards.

The internal ratchet made a space for the pendulum locking bracket on the back plate.

Rapid Recognition Tips
Only this movement has plates of 42mm x 77mm and no ratchet on the back.

The distinctive Koma cut-out in most back plates.

Data
Movement ID Code ...... **KM-MLI**
Plate shape .... **Rectangular**
Plate width **42mm**
Plate height **77mm**
Gap between plates **25mm**
Escapement type .... **Dead beat**
Original key size **3.50mm**
Winding side .... **Right**
Pivot adjuster .... **Screwed bracket**
Locking device: .... **Beneath the base**
Pendulum type/s **4-ball**
Mainspring barrel .... **18mm x 35mm**
Replacement wire .... **No. 12 (Horolovar™ 0.0032"/0.081mm)**
Replacement unit .... **KM-MIN (Horolovar™ 14A)**
Jig settings **98mm, 103mm**
Mainspring .... **15 x 0.50 x 32mm (760mm)**
Beats per minute **8**
Bob weight .... **232g.**

Examples of clocks fitted with the Koma miniature later internal ratchet movement

Manufacturer:
Konrad Mauch

Model:
Koma Midget Early
42mm x 54mm x 20mm

Backplate information:
**Koma beneath a semicircular clock
with hands at 10:12
Made in Germany**

Movement ID code: **KM-MIDGE**

Notes:
This is the early model, with the weaker mainspring. This proved too weak, and later models had a wider barrel, and the gap between the plates increased from 20mm to 21mm.

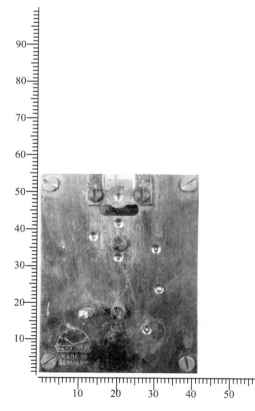

This model has a narrow mainspring barrel.
Note the larger gap between the 14.5mm barrel and the front plate on the early model.

5mm (Wide) Gap

Koma Midget Early
42 x 54 x 20mm

Notes
Lantern cased models may have screwed cases, so a rear hand setter was required. This is a shaft through the hole in the top lefthand corner of the plates, engaging with the motion work.

The hole for the lantern cased hand setter

The adjustable arm is on the front plate. The screwed bracket on the back cannot be used as an adjuster because it is too far from the pallets.

The tubular guard.

Rapid Recognition Tips
Koma plates no longer had the familiar cut-out at the top.

Data
Movement ID Code ...... **KM-MIDGE**
Plate shape .... **Rectangular**
Plate width **42mm**
Plate height **54mm**
Gap between plates **20mm**
Escapement type .... **Pin pallet**
Original key size **2.50mm**
Winding side .... **Left**
Pivot adjuster .... **Adjustable arm**
Locking device: .... **Beneath the base**
Pendulum type/s **3-ball**
Mainspring barrel .... **14.5mm x 26mm**
Replacement wire .... **No. 5 (Horolovar™ 0.0022"/0.056mm)**
Replacement unit .... **KM-MID (Horolovar™ 38A)**
Jig settings **60mm, 65mm**
Mainspring .... **12 x 0.35 x 25mm (700mm)**
Beats per minute **15**
Bob weight .... **90g.**

Examples of clocks fitted with the Koma Midget early movement

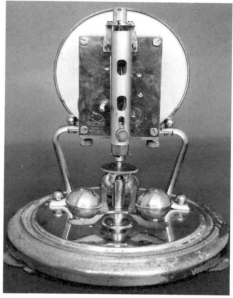

Manufacturer:
Konrad Mauch

Model:
Koma Midget late
42mm x 54mm x 21mm

Backplate information:
**Koma beneath a semicircular clock
        with hands at 10:12
Made in Germany**

Movement ID code: **KM-MIDGL**

Notes:
This is the later model, with the stronger mainspring. The spring in the earlier model proved too weak, and this later model has a wider barrel, and the gap between the plates increased to 21.

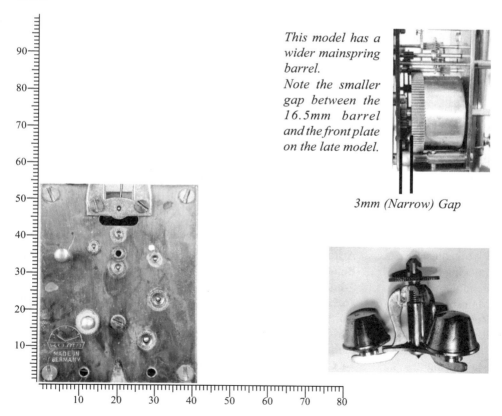

This model has a wider mainspring barrel.
Note the smaller gap between the 16.5mm barrel and the front plate on the late model.

3mm (Narrow) Gap

Koma Midget late
42 x 54 x 21mm

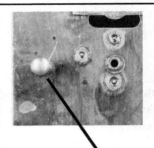

Notes
Lantern cased models may have screwed cases, so a rear hand setter was required. This is a shaft through the hole in the top lefthand corner of the plates, engaging with the motion work.

The knob for the lantern cased hand setter

The adjustable arm is on the front plate. The screwed bracket on the back cannot be used as an adjuster because it is too far from the pallets.

The tubular guard.

Rapid Recognition Tips
Koma plates no longer had the familiar cut-out at the top.

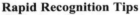

Data
Movement ID Code ...... **KM-MIDGL**
Plate shape .... **Rectangular**
Plate width **42mm**
Plate height **54mm**
Gap between plates **21mm**
Escapement type .... **Pin pallet**
Original key size **2.50mm**
Winding side .... **Left**
Pivot adjuster .... **Adjustable arm**
Locking device: .... **Beneath the base**
Pendulum type/s **3-ball**
Mainspring barrel .... **16.5mm x 26mm**
Replacement wire .... **No. 5 (Horolovar™ 0.0022"/0.056mm)**
Replacement unit .... **KM-MID (Horolovar™ 38A)**
Jig settings **60mm, 65mm**
Mainspring .... **14 x 0.35 x 25mm (700mm)**
Beats per minute **15**
Bob weight .... **90g.**

Examples of clocks fitted with the Koma Midget later movement

J Link & Co

Link started off in partnership with Kern, manufacturing under the name of Kern & Link, but left soon afterwards.

Link resumed independently after the 2nd world war, but only made clocks for a couple of years and few were made.

Although stamped 'Made in Germany', after the war it should have been stamped 'West Germany'.

This early Link has nothing stamped on the back plate, but the name was painted on beneath the base.

J Link listings:

By model:

By Movement Identity Code:

By dimensions:

Rectangular

Manufacturer:
J Link

Model:
Link Standard Narrow
44mm x 95mm x 31mm

Backplate information:
J LINK & CO SCHWENNINGEN
NO (0) JEWELS UNADJUSTED
or
FOUR (4) JEWELS UNADJUSTED

MADE IN GERMANY

Movement ID code: **JL-SN**

Notes:
The four screw holes in the sides were for the wings that importers could add on arrival in the USA. These made the movement look more like a Standard model, without paying the additional import duty.

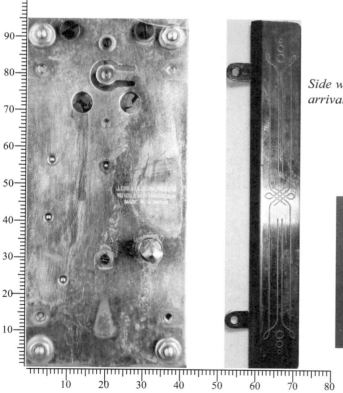

Side wings were fitted on arrival in the USA

17-4 J Link

Link Standard Narrow
44 x 95 x 31mm

Keyhole shaped adjuster arm

Notes
Available in 0 jewels and 4 jewels. The 4 jewel movement was unpopular in the USA because it incurred a higher rate of import duty.

Rapid Recognition Tips
The 'Keyhole' shaped pivot adjuster is unique to J Link.
The wire click spring on the front plate is distinctive.

Data
Movement ID Code	**JL-SN**
Plate shape	**Rectangular**
Plate width	**44mm**
Plate height	**95mm**
Gap between plates	**31mm**
Escapement type	**Dead beat**
Original key size	**4.25**
Winding side	**Right**
Pivot adjuster	**Adjustable arm**
Locking device:	**Guard slider**
Pendulum type/s	**4-ball**
Mainspring barrel	**22mm x 41mm**
Replacement wire	**No.17 (Horolovar™ 0.0037"/0.94mm)**
Replacement unit	**JL-SN (Horolovar™ 16)**
Jig settings	**109mm, 115mm**
Mainspring	**19 x 0.40 x 38mm (1350mm)**
Beats per minute	**8**
Bob weight	**290g.**

The ratchet is on the inside of the front plate but the click spring is on the outside, behind the dial.

Examples of clocks fitted with J Link & Co. movements

Nisshin Clock Industrial Co.

The Nisshin Clock Company of Japan manufactured clocks
under the brand name of Master.

*Nisshin Clock Company
Tokyo Japan*

*MASTER
Nisshin Clock
Industrial Co.
Ltd.*

Nisshin (Master) listings:

By model:

By Movement Identity Code:

By dimensions:

Rectangular
Vest shaped

Manufacturer:
Nisshin Clock Industrial Co.

Model:
Master Standard, round corners
50mm x 91mm x 30mm

Backplate information:
Master with Fleur de Lys above and below the name.
Nisshin Clock Industrial Co. Ltd. Japan

May have a square cut-out at the bottom of the backplate.

Movement ID code: **NC-SR**

Notes:
Distinctive rounded cornered plates. Not to be confused with the model that has square corners.

May have a cut-out in the backplate

Master Standard, round corners
50 x 91 x 30mm

Notes
The escape wheel pivot has an adjustable arm as well as the anchor pivot.

The bob has no hook. It is pinned in position. If you make your own unit, use an inverted top block at the bottom.

Rapid Recognition Tips
Master clocks have nuts on the backplates, unlike the majority of movements which have screws or tapered pins.

The pendulum is pinned in position.

Data
Movement ID Code	**NC-SR**
Plate shape	**Rectangular**
Plate width	**50mm**
Plate height	**91mm**
Gap between plates	**30mm**
Escapement type	**Dead beat**
Original key size	**4.00mm**
Winding side	**Left**
Pivot adjuster	**Adjustable arm**
Locking device:	**Beneath the base**
Pendulum type/s	**4-ball**
Mainspring barrel	**23mm x 44mm**
Replacement wire	**No. 14 (Horolovar™ 0.0034"/0.086mm)**
Replacement unit	**NC-S (Horolovar™ 45A)**
Jig settings	**105mm, 111mm**
Mainspring	**19 x 0.40 x 38mm (1350mm)**
Beats per minute	**8**
Bob weight	**145g.**

Examples of clocks fitted with the Master Standard movement

Manufacturer:
Nisshin Clock Industrial Co.

Model:
Master 100 Day
50mm x 66mm x 21mm

Backplate information:
Nisshin Clock Industrial Co. Ltd. Japan

Movement ID code: **NC-100**

Notes:
Distinctive vest shaped backplate

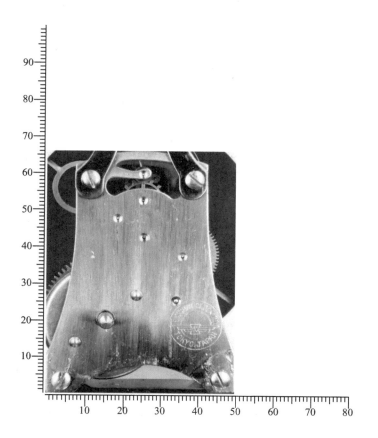

18-8 Master (Nisshin)

Master 100 Day
50 x 66 x 21mm

The pendulum is pinned in position with a grub screw.

Notes

An open loop mainspring, located within a static barrel type cover riveted to the backplate.

Alarm clock style screw on winder with plastic knob and lefthand thread.

The bob has no hook. It is screwed in position. If you make your own unit, use an inverted top block at the bottom.

Rapid Recognition Tips

Loop end spring enclosed in a cover riveted to the backplate.

The loop end spring is inside a cover riveted to the backplate.

Data

Movement ID Code	**NC-100**
Plate shape	**Vest**
Plate width	**50mm**
Plate height	**66mm**
Gap between plates	**21mm**
Escapement type	**Pin Pallet**
Original key size	**Screw on**
Winding side	**Left**
Pivot adjuster	**Adjustable arm**
Locking device:	**Beneath the base**
Pendulum type/s	**4-ball**
Mainspring barrel	**n/a**
Replacement wire	**No. 9 (Horolovar™ 0.0028"/0.071mm)**
Replacement unit	**NC-1 (Horolovar™ 46A)**
Jig settings	**70mm, 76mm**
Mainspring	**10mm loop end**
Beats per minute	**12**
Bob weight	**175g.**

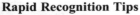

Examples of clocks fitted with the Master 100 day movement

 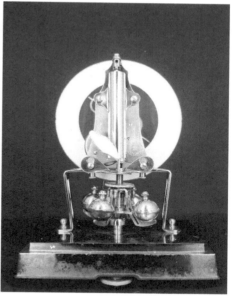

Uhrenfabrik Neueck

Uhrenfabrik Neueck, who had made parts for Herr & Reiner, bought the bankrupt Herr/Reiner factories in 1956, but lasted only about a year.

The majority of their clocks were sold by mail order in the USA, and the main difference between a usual Reiner clock and the Neueck version was the pendulum locking bracket.

If you compare the back plates of the Herr/Reiner Standard Narrow with this movement, you will see that this movement has two holes for a locking bracket at the bottom of the plate. The Herr/Reiner movement had, until the last production, the locking bracket screwed to the underside of the platform.

Technically a clock with the two holes might be a Reiner, but not many were made before Neueck took over.

Neueck listings:

Manufacturer:
Neueck

Model:
Neueck Standard Narrow
44mm x 93mm x 30mm

Backplate information:
**Unmarked or marked
UHRENFABRIK NEUECK GmbH**

Movement ID code: **UN-SNR**

Notes:
The two bracket screws between the corner screws indicate that this was a Neueck clock or possible a late Reiner Clock. By the time these screws were introduced Uhrenfabrik Herr had closed.

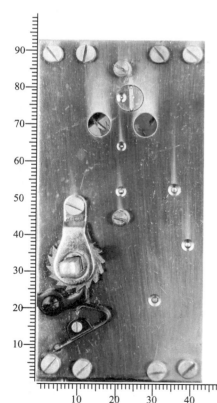

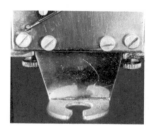

Neueck Standard Narrow
44 x 93 x 30mm

Locking bracket support screws

Notes
The two threaded holes in the bottom of the back plate define this as a Neueck or possibly a very late Reiner clock.
Without those two holes, it is a Herr/Reiner movement.

Rapid Recognition Tips

Data

Movement ID Code	**UN-SN**
Plate shape	**Rectangular**
Plate width	**44mm**
Plate height	**93mm**
Gap between plates	**30mm**
Escapement type	**Dead beat**
Original key size	**4.50mm**
Winding side	**Left**
Pivot adjuster	**Adjustable arm**
Locking device:	**Beneath the base**
Pendulum type/s	**4-ball**
Mainspring barrel	**22mm x 39mm**
Replacement wire	**No.176(Horolovar™ 0.0036"/0.91mm)**
Replacement unit	**UN-SN (Horolovar™ 27C)**
Jig settings	**104mm, 107mm**
Mainspring	**19 x 0.45 x 36mm (1140mm)**
Beats per minute	**8**
Bob weight	**310g.**

Examples of clocks fitted with Neueck Standard narrow movements

Philip Hauck

Philip Hauck manufactured large numbers of quality clocks at the turn of the century, but they bear no logos or stampings apart from serial numbers.

It appears that Charles Terwilliger, author of the Horolovar 400 day Clock Repair Guide, erroneously attributed his clocks to Philip Haas & Co. as there is evidence to suggest that Philip Haas & Co. never manufactured a single Anniversary clock.

Philip Hauck listings:

Manufacturer:
Philip Hauck

Model:
Hauck Standard
66mm x 88mm x 30mm

Backplate information:
May have Germany. Normally a serial number at the bottom of the backplate, adjacent to the ratchet support bracket.

Movement ID code: **PH-STD**

Notes:
Distinctive suspension support that uses two horizontal pins that rest on two arms.

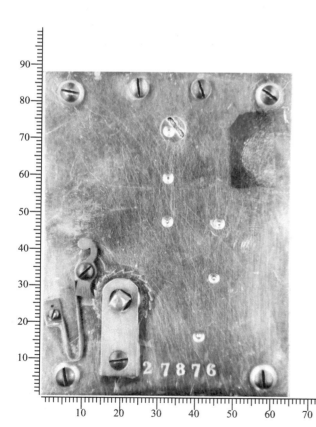

Distinctive support

The typical Hauck narrow gallery pendulum.

Hauck Standard
66 x 88 x 30mm

The two arm support

Notes
The suspension arrangement is quite different to most other clocks, having a two-armed support in which a round bush is fitted. The bush has two pins (actually screws whose heads act as pins) that rest in the arms. The top block fits into the bush. The pins compensate for any tilt forward or back. The bracket has just one fixing screw through the plate, so it can be adjusted to compensate for any lateral tilt. Unfortunately the top block is often missing on clocks that need restoration.

The unique top block, frequently missing.

Rapid Recognition Tips
Distinctive suspension support bracket.
The vertical ratchet wheel bracket is made from solid brass. Most others of this period were flat with a spacing washer and were normally horizontal.

Data

Movement ID Code	**PH-STD**
Plate shape	**Rectangular**
Plate width	**66mm**
Plate height	**88mm**
Gap between plates	**30mm**
Escapement type	**Dead beat**
Original key size	**4.00mm**
Winding side	**Left**
Pivot adjuster	**Eccentric nut**
Locking device:	**None**
Pendulum type/s	**Disc, 4-ball**
Mainspring barrel	**23mm x 39mm**
Replacement wire	**No. 18 (Horolovar™ 0.0038"/0.097mm)**
Replacement unit	**Not readily available**
Jig settings	**4mm, 103mm**
Mainspring	**19 x 0.45 x 36mm (1140mm)**
Beats per minute	**8**
Bob weight	**230g.**

The vertical ratchet wheel bracket made from solid brass.

Examples of clocks fitted with the P. Hauck Standard movement

Schlenker und Posner

For decades 400 day clocks made by Schlenker & Posner were wrongly attributed to both Keieninger & Obergfel and Kern. Due to the similarities between clocks made by these three factories and the frequent absence of any maker's name, differentiating between them can be difficult.

Clocks were made from 1928 - 1938 when the firm was sold to Kern & Sohne. To confuse things further, Kern assembled and sold the remaining stock and some of these were branded 'Kern'.

Schlenker & Posner listings:

Movement Identity Code

Rectangular

Manufacturer:
Schlenker & Posner

Model:
Schlenker & Posner Standard
69mm x 93mm x 30mm

Backplate information:
May have:
A serial number up to around 40,000
SCHLENKER u. POSNER
SCHWENNINGEN
GERMANY

Movement ID code: **SP-STD**

Notes:
The ratchet wheel bridge is made from one flat piece of brass with a washer behind it.

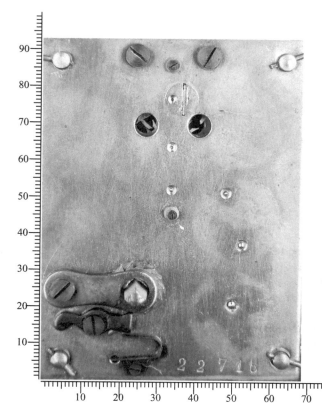

One-piece ratchet wheel bridge

Schlenker & Posner Standard
69 x 93 x 30mm

Notes
Kern and Keinninger & Obergfell both made movements of 69mm x 93mm.

Schlenker & Posner clocks have an external ratchet, but the Kern standard models did not.

Schlenker & Posner movements have inspection holes on both plates. Keininger & Obergfell standard movements also have inspection holes on both plates but the Keininger & Obergfell movement has an adjustable bush on the front plate.

The two inspection holes in the front plate with an unadjustable pivot.

Rapid Recognition Tips
Look for front plate inspection holes on a plate 69mm x 93mm but no adjustable bush on the front plate.

Data
Movement ID Code	**SP-STD**
Plate shape	**Rectangular**
Plate width	**69mm**
Plate height	**93mm**
Gap between plates	**30mm**
Escapement type	**Dead beat**
Original key size	**4.50mm**
Winding side	**Left**
Pivot adjuster	**Eccentric nut**
Locking device:	**None**
Pendulum type/s	**4-ball**
Mainspring barrel	**21mm x 42mm**
Replacement wire	**No. 12 (Horolovar™ 0.0032"/0.081mm)**
Replacement unit	**KO-S (Horolovar™ 1)**
Jig settings	**106mm, 116mm**
Mainspring	**19 x 0.40 x 38mm (1350mm)**
Beats per minute	**8**
Bob weight	**275g.**

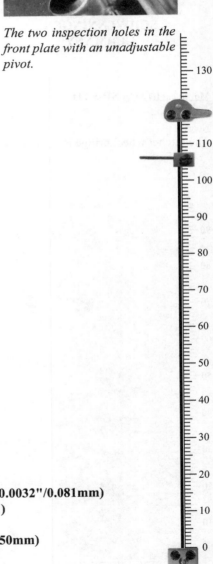

Examples of clocks fitted with the Schlenker & Posner Standard movement.

 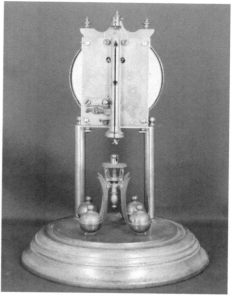

Reinhold Schnekenburger

Reinhold Schnekenburger of Mühlheim made several different models of striking Anniversary clocks in the late 1890's. These clocks are very rare, and were generally in Vienna wall clock cases. The main difference was the escapement. Examples exist of Duplex, Detent and less commonly Crown & Verge.

Despite being well designed and well made, striking 400 day clocks were never popular. The striking easily became out of sequence, and the extra effort needed to trigger the strike each half hour could easily stop a clock that was not in well adjusted. However, there is no doubt that if well adjusted and in the right location, they work reliably.

All the models have the same basic rectangular backplate, except for the upper escapement area.

The firm started in 1882, but was taken over by Müller & Co. when it went bankrupt at the turn of the 19th Century.

Schnekenburger listings:

Serial numbers

It seems that early clocks were made in batches of 30 and the batch number follows the clock serial number on the backplate. This was probably to facilitate matching up the items during assembly without having to note the full serial number.

The batch number can also be found on various parts of the movement, such as the front plate, the winding arbors etc.

As production increased, the batch size increased, and higher batch numbers can be found on later mass produced Vienna regulators etc.

The batch number appears on several parts of the movement.

Manufacturer:
R. Schnekenburger
Mühlhelm

Model:
Schnekenburger Detente
117mm x 122mm x 34mm

Backplate information:
RSM Patent beneath a rose
Serial number & batch number

Movement ID code: **RS-DT**

Notes:

Schnekenburger Detente
117 x 122 x 33mm

Notes

This rare clock strikes the hours and half hours on a gong, and most examples were fitted into gothic Vienna Regulator style cases, although few have survived. Some were mantel clocks under a dome.

The escapement

The pendulum is a 75mm (3") brass ball with four steel rods and vertically adjustable weights.

The escapement is a variant of the Detente escapement.

Rapid Recognition Tips

Unmistakeable rectangular plate.

Countwheel strike

Data

Movement ID Code ...... **RS-DT**
Plate shape .... **Rectangular**
Plate width **117mm**
Plate height **122mm**
Gap between plates **33mm**
Escapement type .... **Detent**
Original key size **4.50mm**
Winding side .... **Front, time and strike**
Pivot adjuster .... **N/A**
Locking device: .... **None**
Pendulum type/s .... **3" (75mm) brass ball**
Mainspring barrel .... **26mm x 56mm**
Replacement wire .... **Case dependant**
Replacement unit .... **None available**
Jig settings .... **Case dependant**

Siegfried Haller

Siegfried Haller made large numbers of Anniversary Clocks in the post war period, but kept to a fairly limited range in terms of appearance.

Early ones were not always marked by name but later examples bear the S. HALLER SIMONSWALD marking.

The Miniature and Midget movements are both the same size. There are two types for each of these movements, so identification of a movement with plates of 44mm x 60mm will require more effort than most other anniversary movements.

The block of text normally found on a Haller movement.

A midget movement is normally screwed to a platform with an integral locking bracket protruding. A miniature has a locking bracket screwed to the lower back-plate, extending downwards by about 20mm.

A Miniature has a screwed bracket. A Midget has a bracket extending from the movement platform.

Siegfried Haller listings:

By model:

By Movement Identity Code:

By dimensions:

Manufacturer:
Siegfried Haller

Model:
Haller Standard Passing Strike
73mm x 85mm x 31mm

Backplate information:
Hasi
Germany

Movement ID code: **SH-PS**

Notes:

This unusual movement has a bell mounted on a curved bracket screwed to the front. A bell hammer is raised by the motion work and strikes once every hour.

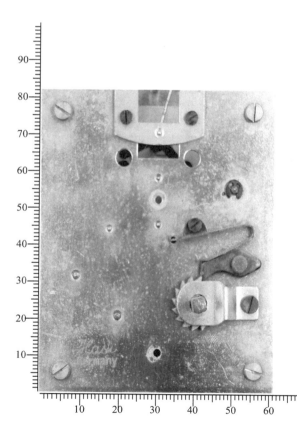

Bell mounted on front pediment.

Haller Standard Passing Strike
73 x 85 x 31mm

Notes
The adjuster is an eccentric nut on the front plate. The position of the screwed bracket is fixed.

Metal base.

Passing strike lever

Rapid Recognition Tips
The split washer that secures the bell hammer arbor is unique to this movement.

The split washer on the bell hammer shaft.

Data

Movement ID Code	**SH-PS**
Plate shape	**Rectangular**
Plate width	**73mm**
Plate height	**85mm**
Gap between plates	**31mm**
Escapement type	**Dead beat**
Original key size	**4.00mm**
Winding side	**Right**
Pivot adjuster	**Eccentric nut (front)**
Locking device:	**None**
Pendulum type/s	**4-ball**
Mainspring barrel	**21.5mm x 41mm**
Replacement wire	**No. 18 (Horolovar™ 0.0030"/0.076mm)**
Replacement unit	**SH-SN (Horolovar™ 42A)**
Jig settings	**113mm, 120mm**
Mainspring	**18 x 0.45 x 38mm (1120mm)**
Beats per minute	**8**
Bob weight	**185g.**

130
120
110
100
90
80
70
60
50
40
30
20
10
0

Examples of clocks fitted with the Haller Standard Passing Strike movement

 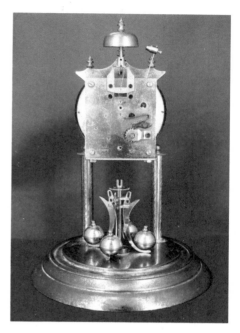

Manufacturer:
Siegfried Haller

Model:
Haller Standard Narrow early
42mm x 84mm x 31mm

Backplate information:
No(0) jewels
Unadjusted
Germany

Movement ID code: **SH-SNE**

Notes:
Not to be confused with the later Siegfried Haller movement that looks similar but has a suspension guard that is fixed with four pegs, and makes considerable use of plastic. This model uses a tubular metal guard.

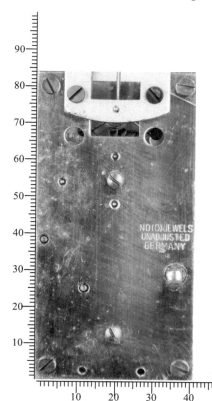

Haller Standard Narrow early
42 x 84 x 31mm

Notes
The adjuster is an eccentric nut on the front plate. The position of the screwed bracket is fixed.

Metal base.

Rapid Recognition Tips

Metal guard fixed with two screws

Data
Movement ID Code ...... **SH-SNE**
Plate shape .... **Rectangular**
Plate width **42mm**
Plate height **84mm**
Gap between plates **31mm**
Escapement type .... **Dead beat**
Original key size **4.00mm**
Winding side .... **Right**
Pivot adjuster.............. **Eccentric nut (front)**
Locking device: .... **Beneath the base**
Pendulum type/s **4-ball**
Mainspring barrel .... **21.5mm x 41mm**
Replacement wire .... **No. 18 (Horolovar™ 0.0030"/0.076mm)**
Replacement unit .... **SH-SN (Horolovar™ 42A)**
Jig settings **113mm, 120mm**
Mainspring .... **18 x 0.45 x 38mm (1120mm)**
Beats per minute **8**
Bob weight .... **185g.**

Examples of clocks fitted with the Haller Standard narrow early movement

Manufacturer:
Siegfried Haller

Model:
Haller Standard Narrow late
42mm x 84mm x 31mm

Backplate information:
S. Haller
Simonswald
No (0) jewels
Unadjusted
Germany

Movement ID code: **SH-SNL**

Notes:
Not to be confused with the earlier Haller movement that looks similar but has a suspension guard that is fixed with two central screws, and uses no plastic. This model makes considerable use of plastic, and in many ways they are of a lower quality than similar models of that period.

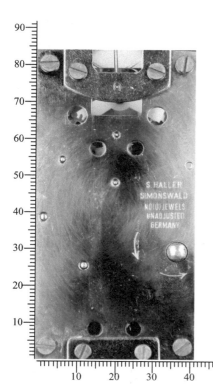

Haller Standard Narrow late
42 x 84 x 31mm

Notes

The adjuster is an adjustable arm on the front plate. The screwed bracket is fixed.

This movement makes considerable use of plastic, and even the escapement is partly made of white plastic.

Distinctive winding direction arrows are often by the right-hand sided winding shaft, probably because this movement winds in an anticlockwise direction, unlike the majority of anniversary clocks.

4 hole push-in guard

Rapid Recognition Tips

Plastic escapement parts.

Data

Movement ID Code	**SH-SNL**
Plate shape	**Rectangular**
Plate width	**42mm**
Plate height	**84mm**
Gap between plates	**31mm**
Escapement type	**Dead beat**
Original key size	**4.00mm**
Winding side	**Right**
Pivot adjuster	**Adjustable arm (front)**
Locking device:	**Beneath the base**
Pendulum type/s	**4-ball**
Mainspring barrel	**21.5mm x 41mm**
Replacement wire	**No. 10 (Horolovar™ 0.003"/0.076mm)**
Replacement unit	**SH-SN (Horolovar™ 42A)**
Jig settings	**108mm, 113mm**
Mainspring	**18 x 0.45 x 38mm (1120mm)**
Beats per minute	**8**
Bob weight	**185g.**

Examples of clocks fitted with the Siegfried Haller Standard Narrow Late movement

Manufacturer:
Siegfried Haller

Model:
Haller Miniature, early
44mm x 60mm x 21mm

Backplate information:
No (0) jewels
Unadjusted
Germany

Movement ID code: **SH-MINE**

Notes:
This is the miniature movement, not to be confused with the midget movement of the same size. This model has no pivot adjuster. **If there is an adjuster on the front plate, it is the late movement.**

A Miniature has a screwed bracket whereas a Midget has a bracket extending from the movement platform.

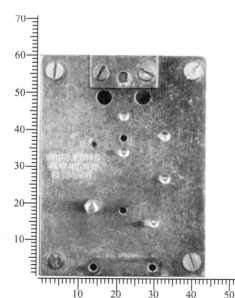

Haller Miniature, early
44 x 60 x 21mm

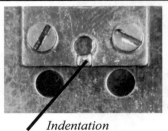

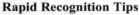 *Indentation*

Notes

A suspension guard is fitted with two centrally placed screws.

The correct pendulum has a square tip, which locates in a square hole in the cup on the base. The pendulum is significantly heavier than the later model.

The top bracket does not have a pivot hole in it and the front pivot is in a fixed bush.

If the platform on which the movement rests has an integral pendulum locking bracket, the clock is a midget.

Rapid Recognition Tips

The only miniature movement that has no pivot adjustment.
This movement has an indentation in the top bracket, to prevent it touching the anchor pivot oil cup.

Data

Movement ID Code ...... **SH-MINE**
Plate shape .... **Rectangular**
Plate width **44mm**
Plate height **60mm**
Gap between plates **21mm**
Escapement type .... **Pin pallet**
Original key size **3.00mm**
Winding side .... **Left**
Pivot adjuster .... **None**
Locking device: .... **Beneath the base**
Pendulum type/s **4-ball**
Mainspring barrel .... **14mm x 27mm**
Replacement wire .... **No. 2 (Horolovar™ 0.019"/0.048mm)**
Replacement unit .... **Unavailable**
Jig settings **77mm, 80mm**
Mainspring .... **12 x 0.40 x 24mm (580mm)**
Beats per minute **6**
Bob weight .... **255g.**

Examples of clocks fitted with the Siegfried Haller Miniature Early movement

Manufacturer:
Siegfried Haller

Model:
Haller Miniature, late
44mm x 60mm x 21mm

Backplate information:
S. Haller
Simonswald
No (0) jewels
Unadjusted
Germany

Movement ID code: **SH-MINL**

Notes:
This is the miniature, not to be confused with the midget movement of the same size. The pendulums are quite different. The adjuster is an adjustable arm on the front plate. **If there is no adjuster on the front plate, it is the early movement.**

This later model now has a pivot arm in the frontplate

A Miniature has a screwed bracket whereas a Midget has a bracket extending from the movement platform.

This model came with different pendulums to accommodate different pillar heights, using different locking brackets and varying length pendulum centre shafts.

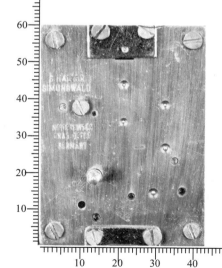

Short pillar pendulum

Tall pillar pendulum

Haller Miniature, late
44 x 60 x 21mm

Notes
Two models exist, one with a plastic guard that pushes into four holes, and another with a guard that is fixed with two screws on the left side.

4 hole push-in guard

Two screw guard

Rapid Recognition Tips

Data
Movement ID Code	**SH-MINL**
Plate shape	**Rectangular**
Plate width	**44mm**
Plate height	**60mm**
Gap between plates	**21mm**
Escapement type	**Pin pallet**
Original key size	**3.00mm**
Winding side	**Left**
Pivot adjuster	**Adjustable arm (front)**
Locking device:	**Beneath the base**
Pendulum type/s	**4-ball**
Mainspring barrel	**14mm x 27mm**
Replacement wire	**No. 1 (Horolovar™ 0.018"/0.046mm)**
Replacement unit	**SH-ML (Horolovar™ 43A)**
Jig settings	**74mm, 78mm**
Mainspring	**12 x 0.40 x 24mm (580mm)**
Beats per minute	**10**
Bob weight	**160g.**

Examples of clocks fitted with the Siegfried Haller Miniature late movement

Manufacturer:
Siegfried Haller

Model:
Haller Midget Early
44mm x 60mm x 21mm

Backplate information:
S. Haller
Simonswald
No (0) jewels
Unadjusted
Germany

Movement ID code: **SH-MIDGE**

Notes:
This is the midget, not to be confused with the miniature of the same size. The pendulums are quite different, and on the this model the whole pendulum is only 40mm high.
Two versions exist. This early one has the rear pallet pivot in the backplate. The later one has the pivot in a fixed screwed bracket.

A Midget has a bracket extending from the movement platform while a Miniature has a screwed bracket .

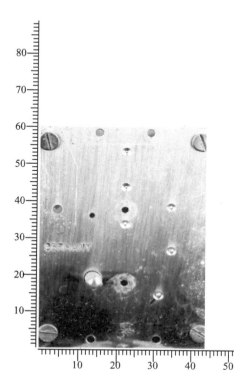

Note that the top of the plate has no cutout, and the pivot is held by a conventional pivot hole.

Haller Midget Early
44 x 60 x 21mm

Notes

The adjuster is an adjustable arm on the front plate. The screwed bracket on the later version is fixed.

This later model has a centrally screwed metal guard. Irritatingly for repairers, it has no facility for refitting without completely removing the screws, and has loose spacer washers beneath. Better designed guards can be slipped over the screw heads. As a result, many are missing.

The screwed guard.

Rapid Recognition Tips

A midget can be distinguished from a miniature by the shorter distance between the suspension bracket and the pendulum hook of 70mm. A miniature is 90mm.

Data

Movement ID Code ...... **SH-MIDGE**
Plate shape .... **Rectangular**
Plate width **44mm**
Plate height **60mm**
Gap between plates **21mm**
Escapement type .... **Pin pallet**
Original key size **3.00mm**
Winding side .... **Left**
Pivot adjuster .... **Adjustable arm (front)**
Locking device: .... **Beneath the base**
Pendulum type/s **4-ball**
Mainspring barrel .... **14mm x 27mm**
Replacement wire .... **No. 1 (Horolovar™ 0.018"/0.046mm)**
Replacement unit .... **SH-MIDG (Horolovar™ 44A)**
Jig settings **57mm, 60mm**
Mainspring .... **12 x 0.40 x 24mm (580mm)**
Beats per minute **10**
Bob weight .... **125g.**

Examples of clocks fitted with the Siegfried Haller Midget early movement

Manufacturer:
Siegfried Haller

Model:
Haller Midget Late
44mm x 60mm x 21mm

Backplate information:
S. Haller
Simonswald
No (0) jewels
Unadjusted
Germany

Movement ID code: **SH-MIDGL**

Notes:
This is the midget, not to be confused with the miniature of the same size. The pendulums are quite different, and on the this model the whole pendulum is only 40mm high.
Two versions exist. This late one has the rear pallet pivot in a fixed screwed bracket. The earlier version has the pivot in a hole in the back plate.

A Midget has a bracket extending from the movement platform while a Miniature has a screwed bracket .

Note that the top of the plate is cut away to allow the pivot to be held by a fixed screwed bracket.

Haller Midget Late
44 x 60 x 21mm

Notes
The adjuster is an adjustable arm on the front plate. The screwed bracket on this later version is fixed.

This later model has a plastic suspension guard fitted with two side screws. It can be removed and replaced more easily than the early metal guard.

'Two side screw' guard

Rapid Recognition Tips
A midget can be distinguished from a midget by the shorter distance between the suspension bracket and the pendulum hook of 70mm. A miniature is 90mm.

Data
Movement ID Code	**SH-MIDGL**
Plate shape	**Rectangular**
Plate width	**44mm**
Plate height	**60mm**
Gap between plates	**21mm**
Escapement type	**Pin pallet**
Original key size	**3.00mm**
Winding side	**Left**
Pivot adjuster	**Adjustable arm (front)**
Locking device:	**Beneath the base**
Pendulum type/s	**4-ball**
Mainspring barrel	**14mm x 27mm**
Replacement wire	**No. 1 (Horolovar™ 0.018"/0.046mm)**
Replacement unit	**SH-MIDG (Horolovar™ 44A)**
Jig settings	**57mm, 60mm**
Mainspring	**12 x 0.40 x 24mm (580mm)**
Beats per minute	**10**
Bob weight	**125g.**

Examples of clocks fitted with the Siegfried Haller Midget late movement

Manufacturer:
Siegfried Haller

Model:
Haller Reverse wound
65mm x 102mm x 30mm

Backplate information:
S. HALLER
MADE IN GERMANY
ONE (1)JEWEL
UNADJUSTED

Movement ID code: **SH-GTB**

Notes:
This most unusual anniversary clock can explode, normally causing serious damage to itself and possible injury to anyone close to it.

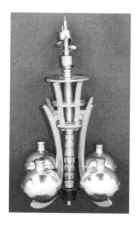

Haller Reverse Wound
65 x 102 x 30mm

Notes

This unusual Anniversary clock has been nicknamed 'The German Time Bomb' because it normally ticks away happily for years, but suddenly and without any warning, its toothless ratchet can slip and the mainspring will unwind noisily. It can destroy itself in the process, and can cause injury to anyone near it at the time. It can shatter its own dome as it explodes.

It is an extremely dangerous clock and you should consider very carefully before putting it on public or domestic display unless you are sure it is unwound and that it will remain so.

Rapid Recognition Tips

This clock has so many unique features it is instantly recognisable. The most obvious features are:
The skeletonised train on the front plate.
The shape of the backplate.

Data

Movement ID Code	**SH-GTB**
Plate shape	**Rectangular**
Plate width	**65mm**
Plate height	**102mm**
Gap between plates	**30mm**
Escapement type	**Pin pallet**
Original key size	**6.00mm**
Winding side	**Centre**
Pivot adjuster..............	**n/a**
Locking device:	**None**
Pendulum type/s	**4-ball**
Mainspring barrel	**n/a**
Replacement wire	**n/a**
Replacement unit	**n/a**
Jig settings	**n/a**
Mainspring	**24 x 0.30 x 5,500mm, naturally coiled**
Beats per minute	**12**
Bob weight	**50g.**

Examples of clocks fitted with the Haller Reverse Wound movement

SAFETY WARNING

If you are considering working on the movement, either to service or repair it, you need to be aware that this clock was not nicknamed 'The German Time Bomb' as a term of endearment but because it can and does cause injury without any warning, and it can do so at any time, ticking or not.

If you are not an experienced clock repairer, do not attempt to work on it. Put it in a strong carton, cover it with an old towel, seal the box and mark the box appropriately.

Store it away from children.

Most accidents occur when owners unwittingly undo the four screws on the back plate, expecting to find some sort of clock mechanism inside, but releasing a 5.5 metre long and very sharp mainspring.

Do not undo these screws unless you know that the mainspring has been let down fully.

*Do **not** start dismantling by undoing these screws on the back. If you do, the clock may explode.*

Gebrüder Staiger

Gebr. Staiger of St. Georgen, Germany went on to produce very large numbers of battery and quartz clocks, but their early clocks were mechanical.

At first glance they don't appear to warrant a place in this book, but examination will show they are ingenious torsion clocks, albeit only 8-day.

Staiger listings:

Manufacturer:
Gebr. Staiger

Model:
Staiger Round
60mm

Backplate information:
Unmarked or may have
GEBR. STAIGER
N0 (0) JEWELS UNADJUSTED

Movement ID code: **GS-60**

Notes:
Timekeeping adjustments are made using the knurled thumb wheel on the pendulum located inside the base.

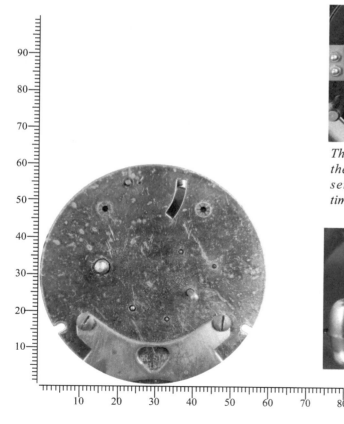

The real pendulum is inside the base. Use the central serrated wheel to adjust timekeeping.

Staiger
60mm

Notes
Open spring 8-day torsion movement. Unlike other 'novelty' clocks of the time, this movement still uses the pendulum for timekeeping. However the pendulum you see is a lightweight plastic one attached to the torsion wire. The real pendulum is beneath the base, similar to the Kaiser Globe.

A lever is provided on some models that 'kick-starts' the bob on the base.

The suspension wire hangs on a sprung top block, making it much more portable.

Rapid Recognition Tips
Small round 8-day movement.

Some models are fitted with a lever which gently kick-starts the internal disc pendulum.

Data
Movement ID Code	**GS-60**
Plate shape	**Round**
Plate width	**60mm**
Plate height	**60mm**
Gap between plates	**11mm**
Escapement type	**Pin pallet**
Original key size	**Fitted winder**
Winding side	**Left**
Pivot adjuster	**N/A**
Locking device:	**None**
Pendulum type/s	**Visible 4-ball, internal disc**
Mainspring barrel	**N/A**
Replacement wire	**N/A**
Replacement unit	**N/A**
Jig settings	**N/A**
Mainspring	**loop end 600 x x 0.40mm x 500mm**
Beats per minute	**30**
Bob weight	**N/A**

Examples of clocks fitted with the Staiger 60mm Round movement

Uhrenfabrik Herr
&
Uhrenfabrik Reiner

These two firms were not financially connected or under the same ownership or management, but the similarity of the products and interchangeability of the parts indicates that they worked very closely

together. So much so that their listings have been combined in this book to avoid confusion and duplication. It is thought that the two owning families were related.

Examples do appear with Herr stamped on the plates, but the majority of sales were to importers in the USA who opted to have their own brand names stamped on the plates. Examples include Forrestville and Euramca.

Parts were also made for them by Uhrenfabrik Neueck, and when Herr & Reiner closed, Neueck continued to make clocks using the final design.

Uhrenfabrik Herr & Reiner listings:

Manufacturer:

Uhrenfabrik Herr/Reiner

Backplate information:

May have:
Uhrenfabrik Herr K.G.
Gûtenbach
No (0) JEWELS UNADJUSTED
MADE IN GERMANY
GERMANY

Model:

Herr/Reiner Standard
Clockwise adjuster
66mm x 88mm x 30mm

Movement ID code: **HR-STD**

Notes:
Sometimes found with no maker's name or Germany in an arc. Not to be confused with the Jahresuhrenfabrik Standard of the same plate size, as almost all the parts are similar. Uhrenfabrik Herr and Uhrenfabrik Reiner worked closely together and some parts frequently appear to have been made from the same tooling.

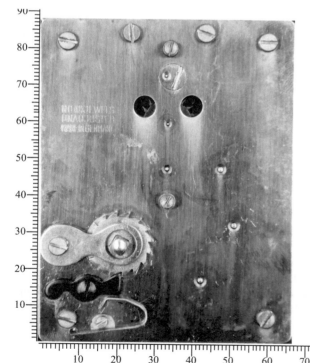

25-4 U. Herr/Reiner

Herr/Reiner Standard
Clockwise adjuster
66mm x 88mm x 30mm

Notes

This model may have a pendulum with a screw threaded adjuster that has to be turned clockwise to make it go faster. Most 400 day clocks are adjusted in the opposite direction. Beneath the base the locking lever is slightly more complicated than the average clock on later models.

It is so similar to the Jahresuhrenfabrik A. Schatz Standard that it even has spacers between the platform and the movement, rarely seen on these clocks. However, these have screwed plates.

Clockwise adjuster

Rapid Recognition Tips

1: 66mm x 88mm plate with rounded corners, secured with screws not pins.

2: Locking bracket screwed to the underside of the platform on later models.

Data

Movement ID Code	**HR-STD**
Plate shape	**Rectangular**
Plate width	**66mm**
Plate height	**88mm**
Gap between plates	**30mm**
Escapement type	**Dead Beat**
Original key size	**4.50mm**
Winding side	**Left**
Pivot adjuster	**Eccentric nut**
Locking device:	**Beneath the base**
Pendulum type/s	**4-ball**
Mainspring barrel	**22mm x 39mm**
Replacement wire	**No. 19 (Horolovar™ 0.0040"/0.102mm)**
Replacement unit	**HR-ST (Horolovar™ 27A)**
Jig settings	**102mm, 108mm**
Mainspring	**19 x 0.45 x 36mm (1140mm)**
Beats per minute	**8**
Bob weight	**310g.**

Bracket screwed to the platform on later models.

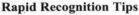

Examples of clocks fitted with the Herr Standard movement.

Manufacturer:
Uhrenfabrik Herr/Reiner

Backplate information:
May have:
Uhrenfabrik Herr K.G.
Gûtenbach
No (0) JEWELS UNADJUSTED
MADE IN GERMANY

Model:
Herr/Reiner Standard Narrow
Clockwise adjuster
44mm x 93mm x 30mm

Movement ID code: **HR-SNR**

Notes:
Sometimes found with no maker's name, or with an importer's mark such as the Cuckoo
Clock Mfg Co., Euramca Trading Corp., Forestville etc.
This is the common early model that has no bracket screws in the bottom of the back plate.
Movements with those screws are listed in the Neueck section, being made by them or by
Reiner during their final months.

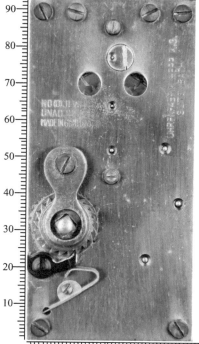

*Not to be confused with the movement that
has two bracket support screws between the
bottom corner screws.*

Herr/Reiner Standard Narrow
Clockwise adjuster
44mm x 93mm x 30mm

Notes

This model has a pendulum with a screw threaded adjuster that has to be turned clockwise to make it go faster. Most 400 day clocks are adjusted in the opposite direction. Beneath the base the locking lever is slightly more complicated than the average clock.

Clockwise adjuster

Rapid Recognition Tips

1: Locking bracket screwed to the underside of the platform.

Data

Movement ID Code ...... **HR-SNR**
Plate shape .... **Rectangular**
Plate width **44mm**
Plate height **93mm**
Gap between plates **30mm**
Escapement type .... **Dead Beat**
Original key size **4.50mm**
Winding side .... **Left**
Pivot adjuster .... **Eccentric nut**
Locking device: .... **Beneath the base**
Pendulum type/s **4-ball**
Mainspring barrel .... **22mm x 39mm**
Replacement wire .... **No. 18 (Horolovar™ 0.0038"/0.097mm)**
Replacement unit .... **HR-SN (Horolovar™ 27B)**
Jig settings **103mm, 110mm**
Mainspring .... **19 x 0.45 x 36mm (1140mm)**
Beats per minute **8**
Bob weight .... **200g.**

Examples of clocks fitted with the Herr/Reiner Standard Narrow (clockwise) movement.

Manufacturer:
Uhrenfabrik Herr &
Uhrenfabrik M. Reiner

Model:
Herr/Reiner Miniature Early
44mm x 70mm x 23mm

Backplate information:
NO (0) JEWELS
UNADJUSTED
MADE IN GERMANY
Normally unbranded, but may be
marked Euramca Trading, or
Uhrenfabrik Herr or Forrestville

Movement ID code: **HR-MINE**

Notes:
This is the early model, with the top suspension guard screw <u>above</u> the anchor pivot hole.

Note that the top guard screw is <u>above</u> the anchor pivot hole on the early model

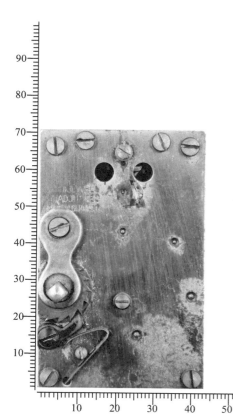

Herr/Reiner Miniature Early
44 x 70 x 23mm

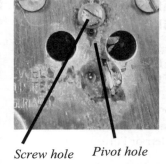

Notes
It is important to verify the position of the upper screw hole on the guard relative to the anchor pivot hole (the top pivot hole).

On this early model the screw is above the pivot hole.

Some were fitted with plate extensions to take advantage of an outdated US customs rule.

Screw hole   *Pivot hole*

Rapid Recognition Tips
This and the other 44mm x 70mm Reiner movements have their vertical ratchet wheel bracket more than half way up the side of the backplate.

Note the gap between the platform and the plates.

Distinctive gap between the platform and the plates

Data

Movement ID Code	**HR-MINE**
Plate shape	**Rectangular**
Plate width	**44mm**
Plate height	**70mm**
Gap between plates	**23mm**
Escapement type	**Dead Beat**
Original key size	**4.00mm**
Winding side	**Right**
Pivot adjuster	**Eccentric nut**
Locking device:	**Beneath the base**
Pendulum type/s	**4-ball**
Mainspring barrel	**19mm x 39mm**
Replacement wire	**No. 10 (Horolovar™ 0.0025"/0.064mm)**
Replacement unit	**HR-ME (Horolovar™ 28B)**
Jig settings	**82mm, 88mm**
Mainspring	**16 x 0.45 x 36mm (1040mm)**
Beats per minute	**8**
Bob weight	**166g.**

With and without plate extensions.

Examples of clocks fitted with the Herr/Reiner miniature early movement

Manufacturer:
Uhrenfabrik Herr &
Uhrenfabrik M. Reiner

Model:
Herr/Reiner Miniature Late
(10" dome)
44mm x 70mm x 23mm

Backplate information:
NO (0) JEWELS
UNADJUSTED
MADE IN GERMANY
Normally unbranded, but may be marked
Euramca Trading, or Uhrenfabrik Herr or
Forrestville

Movement ID code: **HR-ML10**

Notes:
This is the later model, with the top suspension guard screw <u>below</u> the anchor pivot hole
.

**This information applies to this movement when used in a standard clock with a 10"
(250mm) dome, but not when used in the miniature clock under an 8" (200mm) dome.**

*Note that the top guard
screw is <u>below</u> the anchor
pivot hole on the late model*

**Herr/Reiner Miniature Late
(10" dome)
44 x 70 x 23mm**

Notes
It is important to verify the position of the upper screw hole on the guard relative to the anchor pivot hole (the top pivot hole).

Screw hole   Pivot hole

On this later model the screw is below the pivot hole.

Note the gap between the platform and the movement.

Distinctive gap between the platform and the plates

Rapid Recognition Tips
This and the other 44mm x 70mm Reiner movements have their ratchet wheel bracket more than half way up the side of the backplate.

Note the gap between the platform and the plates.

Data

Movement ID Code	**HR-ML10**
Plate shape	**Rectangular**
Plate width	**44mm**
Plate height	**70mm**
Gap between plates	**23mm**
Escapement type	**Dead Beat**
Original key size	**4.00mm**
Winding side	**Right**
Pivot adjuster	**Eccentric nut**
Locking device:	**Beneath the base**
Pendulum type/s	**4-ball**
Mainspring barrel	**19mm x 39mm**
Replacement wire	**No. 12 (Horolovar™ 0.0032"/0.081mm)**
Replacement unit	**HR-MLL (Horolovar™ 23A)**
Jig settings	**93mm, 101mm**
Mainspring	**16 x 0.45 x 36mm (1040mm)**
Beats per minute	**8**
Bob weight	**266g.**

Examples of clocks fitted with the Herr/Reiner miniature late movement under 10" dome

Manufacturer:
Uhrenfabrik Herr &
Uhrenfabrik M. Reiner

Model:
Herr/Reiner Miniature Late
8" (200mm) dome
44mm x 70mm x 23mm

Backplate information:
NO (0) JEWELS
UNADJUSTED
MADE IN GERMANY
Normally unbranded, but may be marked
Euramca Trading, or Uhrenfabrik Herr or
Forrestville

Movement ID code: **HR-ML8**

Notes:
This is the miniature model, with the top suspension guard screw <u>below</u> the anchor pivot
hole. **This information applies to this movement when used in a miniature clock with
an 8" (200mm) dome, but not when used in the standard clock under a 10" (250mm)
dome.**

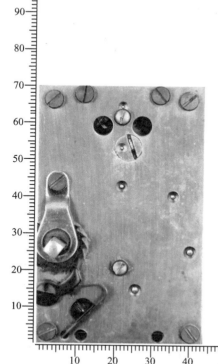

*Note that the top guard screw
is below the anchor pivot
hole on the late model*

**Herr/Reiner Miniature Late
8" (200mm) dome
44 x 70 x 23mm**

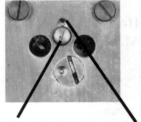

Notes
It is important to verify the position of the upper screw hole on the guard relative to the anchor pivot hole (the top pivot hole).

Screw hole   Pivot hole

On this later model the screw is below the pivot hole.

On the 8" (200mm) dome model there is no gap between the platform and the movement

On the 8" dome model there is no gap between the platform and the movement

Rapid Recognition Tips
This and the other 44mm x 70mm Reiner movements have their ratchet wheel bracket more than half way up the side of the backplate.
Note the lack of gap between the platform and the plates.

Data
Movement ID Code	**HR-ML8**
Plate shape	**Rectangular**
Plate width	**44mm**
Plate height	**70mm**
Gap between plates	**23mm**
Escapement type	**Dead Beat**
Original key size	**4.00mm**
Winding side	**Right**
Pivot adjuster..............	**Eccentric nut**
Locking device:	**Beneath the base**
Pendulum type/s	**4-ball**
Mainspring barrel	**19mm x 39mm**
Replacement wire	**No. 9 (Horolovar™ 0.0028"/0.071mm)**
Replacement unit	**HR-MLS (Horolovar™ 28C**
Jig settings	**82mm, 88mm**
Mainspring	**16 x 0.45 x 36mm (1039mm)**
Beats per minute	**8**
Bob weight	**275g.**

Examples of clocks fitted with the Herr/Reiner miniature late movement under 8" dome

W. A. Shmid-Schlenker Jr.
GmbH & Co. KG

Shmid-Schlenker started out in 1935 in Schwenningen, Germany and later moved to Bad Durheim.

They manufactured small antique style clocks including Anniversary Clocks. Many were pretty bedroom style clocks. They closed in the 1970's.

Shmid-Schlenker listings:

By model:

By Movement Identity Code

Rectangular
Round

Manufacturer:
W.u A. Shmid-Schlenker Jr.

Model:
Shmid-Schlenker Large Spring
87mm x 44mm

Backplate information:

W.& A. SHMID-SCHLENKER jr.
GERMANY
7 (SEVEN) JEWELS UNADJUSTED
DBP angem

Movement ID code: **SS-LS**

Notes:

Not a true torsion movement, but a hairspring in the escapement, complete with screw index adjuster, controls the rotation. Unlike other smaller Shmid-Schlenker models, this clock goes for a year, driven by a massive mainspring.

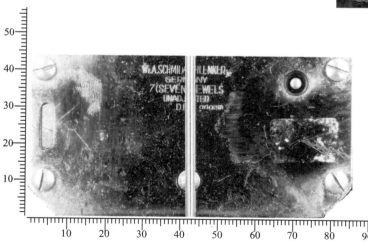

Shmid-Schlenker
87 mm x 44mm

Notes
The dancers forming the bob rotate on a jewelled vertical shaft. A jewelled platform escapement drives the pendulum. The platform lever that would normally drive a balance wheel side to side in a conventional clock gives this clock's pendulum a delicate push.

This is a triple plate movement. The spring barrel and 1st wheel are mounted between the backplate and the centre plate. Everything else is mounted between the centre plate and the front plate.

A cap in the dial hides the front winding hole.

Rapid Recognition Tips
The 65mm barrel is the largest barrel you will see on a 400 Day Clock

Winding hole disguised by a cap.

Data
Movement ID Code	**SS-LS**
Plate shape	**Rectangular**
Plate width	**87mm**
Plate height	**44mm**
Gap between plates	**23mm, 10mm**
Escapement type	**Lever escapement**
Original key size	**5.25mm**
Winding side	**Front, Central**
Pivot adjuster	**n/a**
Locking device:	**None**
Pendulum type/s	**2 dancers**
Mainspring barrel	**23mm x 65mm**
Replacement wire	**n/a**
Replacement unit	**n/a**
Jig settings	**n/a**
Mainspring	**n/a**
Beats per minute	**12**
Bob weight	**n/a**

Examples of clocks fitted with the Shmid-Schlenker Large Spring movement.

Manufacturer:
W.u A. Shmid-Schlenker Jr.

Model:
Shmid-Schlenker
55 mm round, open spring

Backplate information:
W.u. A. SHMID-SCHLENKER jr.
No (0) JEWELS UNADJUSTED

Movement ID code: **SS-MB**

Notes:
Not a true torsion movement, but a hairspring in the base, complete with index adjuster, controls the rotation. Normally installed upside down, as it was probably a modified balance wheel movement, converted into a pendulum clock.

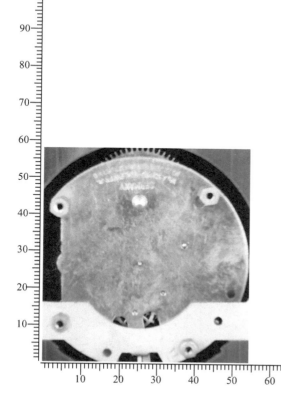

Shmid-Schlenker
55 mm round

Notes
The bob has a single vertical pin at the top, driven by the movement fork. A hairspring with an index lever just above the base controls the speed.

Many examples have a drawer which triggers a miniature music box movement.

Alarm clock style winder and setter.

Rapid Recognition Tips

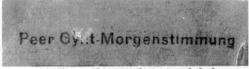

Typical music box tune label

Data

Movement ID Code	**SS-MB**
Plate shape	**Circular**
Plate width	**55mm**
Plate height	**n/a**
Gap between plates	**n/a**
Escapement type	**Pin pallet**
Original key size	**Screw-on alarm style winder**
Winding side	**Central**
Pivot adjuster	**n/a**
Locking device:	**None**
Pendulum type/s	**4-ball**
Mainspring barrel	**Open loop**
Replacement wire	**n/a**
Replacement unit	**n/a**
Jig settings	**n/a**
Mainspring	**n/a**
Beats per minute	**n/a**
Bob weight	**20g.**

Examples of clocks fitted with the Shmid-Schlenker 55mm movement.

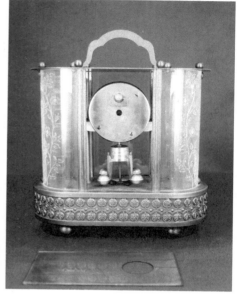

Manufacturer:
W.u A. Shmid-Schlenker Jr.

Model:
Shmid-Schlenker
Uni-directional

Backplate information:
Normally unmarked

Movement ID code: **SS-ES**

Notes:

Not a true torsion movement, but an 8 day movement using a balance wheel. The pendulum is driven in one continuous direction by the train.

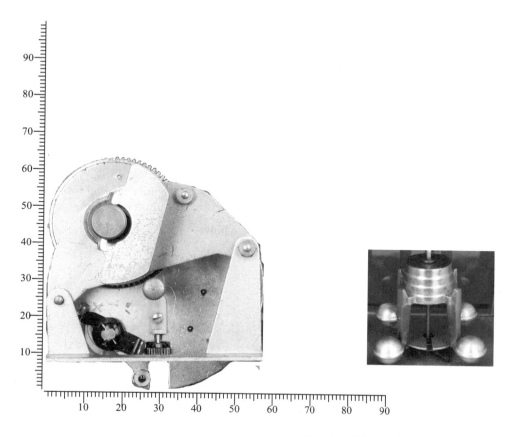

Shmid-Schlenker
Uni-directional, enclosed spring

Notes

The bob has a fine spring steel wire pointing upwards. A gear wheel turns above the pendulum shaft, and the spring catches in the teeth of the gear. Being delicate, the fine spring wire flexes, converting the jerky movement of the gearwheel into the almost continuous rotation of the bob.

Rapid Recognition Tips

The fine spring that drives the pendulum, coiled around the shaft and engaging with the teeth of a gear..

Data

Movement ID Code ...... **SS-ES**
Plate shape .... **Circular**
Plate width **55mm**
Plate height .... **n/a**
Gap between plates **12mm**
Escapement type .... **Balance wheel**
Original key size .... **Screw on alarm style winder**
Winding side .... **left**
Pivot adjuster .... **n/a**
Locking device: .... **None**
Pendulum type/s **4-ball**
Mainspring barrel .... **15mm x 30mm**
Replacement wire .... **n/a**
Replacement unit .... **n/a**
Jig settings .... **n/a**
Mainspring .... **n/a**
Beats per minute **1**
Bob weight .... **20g.**

Examples of clocks fitted with the Shmid-Schlenker unidirectional movement.

W Petersen

W. Petersen of Schwenningen did not trade for long and closed in the early 1950's.

Petersen also sold movements to J. Kaiser, wh stamped the Kaiser name and address on the back plate.

Petersen listings:

By model:

By Movement Identity Code:

By dimensions:
Rectangular

Manufacturer:
W. Petersen

Model:
Petersen Standard
67mm x 89mm x 33mm

Backplate information:
May have:
W. PETERSEN
SCHWENNINGEN/N.
GERMANY
No(0) JEWELS UNADJUSTED
MADE IN GERMANY

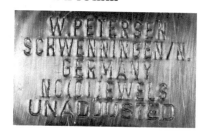

Movement ID code: **WP-STD**

Notes:

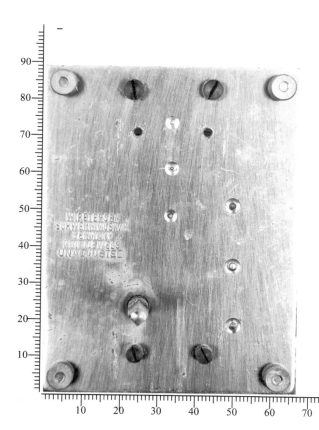

Petersen Standard
67mm x 89mm x 33mm

Dial secured by washers

Notes

The original suspension has a fork that is screwed to a plate, meaning that the suspension wire and the top block are no longer at right angles to the plates. The support can be rotated 90 degrees to accommodate a conventional suspension unit if the fork is lost.

The pivot is adjusted by a small bracket screwed to the front plate.

Back plate secured by serrated nuts.

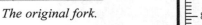

Rapid Recognition Tips

The backplate is secured by serrated brass nuts, not pins.

The dial is secured by three washers, not pins

The original fork.

Data

Movement ID Code	**WP-STD**
Plate shape	**Rectangular**
Plate width	**67mm**
Plate height	**89mm**
Gap between plates	**33mm**
Escapement type	**Dead Beat**
Original key size	**4.00mm**
Winding side	**Left**
Pivot adjuster	**Screwed bracket (front)**
Locking device:	**None**
Pendulum type/s	**4-ball**
Mainspring barrel	**22mm x 42mm**
Replacement wire	**No. 13 (Horolovar™ 0.0033"/0.084mm)**
Replacement unit	**WP-S (Horolovar™ 18C)**
Jig settings	**119mm, 124mm**
Mainspring	**19 x 0.40 x 40mm (1550mm)**
Beats per minute	**8**
Bob weight	**260g.**

Examples of clocks fitted with the Petersen Standard movement.

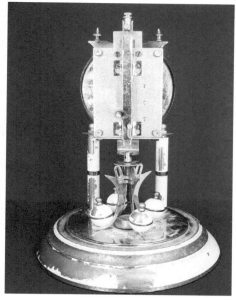

Wintermantel Uhrenfabrik

The Wintermantel Uhrenfabrik in this section must not be confused with Gersen Wintermantel, one of the founders of Jahresuhrenfabrik Schatz.

This section refers to the Gebr. Wintermantel Clock Factory of Triberg, a clock factory set up after the First World War by Albert Wintermantel.

They made 400 day clocks in small quantities between the two world wars but carried on general clock production until the 1950's.

It is common to see them with marble or coloured alabaster bases rather than the typical spun brass bases used by most other factories.

Wintermantel listings:

By model:

By Movement Identity Code:

By dimensions:
Rectangular

Notes:

Manufacturer:
Wintermantel

Model:
Wintermantel Standard
68mm x 88mm x 30mm

Backplate information:

Unmarked
or
W
within a semi-circular escape
wheel

Movement ID code: **WU-STD**

Notes:

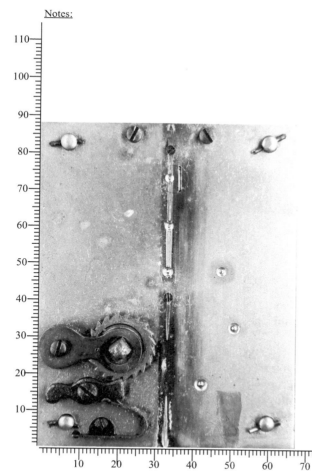

The locking pendulum
adjuster.

Wintermantel Standard
68mm x 88mm x 30mm

Notes
This model bears remarkable similarities to the Jahresuhrenfabrik Standard Early movement and may have bought from them or made from their plans when the patent expired.

Unlike almost every other ball pendulum of its time, this one is adjusted by turning the lower shaft. A small locking screw prevents it from moving. The only other common ones of this style were made by Gustav Becker and Badische.

Many factories used circular suspension guards, but the Wintermantel guard looks like no other.

Rapid Recognition Tips
Distinctive suspension guard.
Pendulum adjuster is the lower shaft.

Data

Movement ID code	**WU-STD**
Plate shape	**Rectangular**
Plate width	**68mm**
Plate height	**88mm**
Gap between plates	**30mm**
Escapement type	**Dead beat**
Original key size	**4.00mm**
Winding side	**Left**
Pivot adjuster	**Eccentric nut**
Locking device:	**None**
Pendulum type/s	**Disc**
Mainspring barrel	**24mm x 39mm**
Replacement wire	**No. 20 (Horolovar™ 0.004"/0.102mm)**
Replacement unit	**JS-S (Horolovar™ 6789)**
Jig settings	**107mm, 114mm**
Mainspring	**19 x 0.45 x 36mm (1145mm)**
Beats per minute	**8**
Bob weight	**315g.**

Examples of clocks fitted with the Gebr. Wintermantel movement

W. Würth & Co

Wilhelm Würth is a lesser known manufacturer of these clocks, probably because it has always been difficult to identify the ones Würth & Co made. The factory was in Schwenninngen, Germany.

There is no known logo and identification normally has to be done on the basis of probability.

The identification suggestions on the following pages are only guides to the likelihood that Wurth & Co was the maker. Other firms used the same pendulum, and others were stamped with the D.R.P number etc.

You need to establish that the clock has no characteristics that indicate it was made by anyone else and then match up as many of the features described here and make your decision.

W. Würth & Co listings:

Manufacturer:
WWürth & Co

Model:
Würth Standard
66mm x 87mm x 30mm

Backplate information:
D. R. P. 144687
made in Germany

Movement ID code: **WW-STD**

The Wurth Gimbal

Notes:
The back plate looks almost identical to the Jahresuhrenfabrik equivalent. This is because Würth copied their clock design when the patent expired. However you will notice that the tail of the click spring does not locate into a hole in the plate.

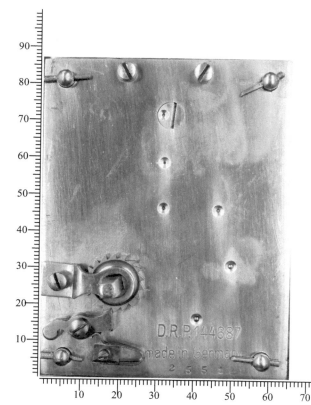

The tail of the click spring does not locate in a hole in the plate.

29-4 W Würth & Co

Würth Standard
66 x 87 x 30mm

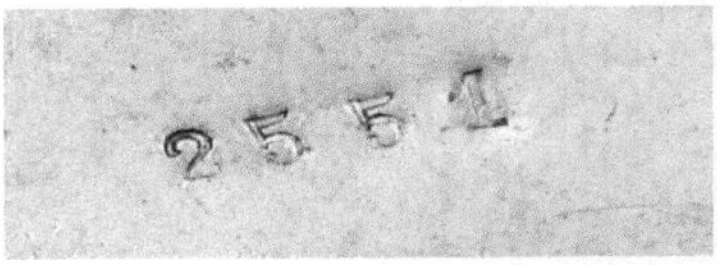

The serial number is normally stamped on the bob.

Notes

The majority of Würth clocks have the 'Snakes & Balls' pendulum shown on the previous page or a bi-metallic strip type. Check that the serial numbers match.
The base is normally ornate when compared to other makes.

Later models had a bridge on the front plate for the escape wheel pivot

Rapid Recognition Tips

There is normally nothing immediately obvious that confirms a Würth clock. You need to look at many features before making a decision.

The base is normally more ornate than Jahresuhrenfabrik clocks.

Data

Movement ID Code...... **WW-STD**
Plate shape.................... **Rectangular**
Plate width.................... **66mm**
Plate height................... **87mm**
Gap between plates **30mm**
Escapement type........... **Dead Beat**
Original key size **4.00mm**
Winding side .... **Left**
Pivot adjuster.............. **Eccentric nut**
Locking device: .... **None**
Pendulum type/s .... **Disc**
Mainspring barrel .... **23mm x 40mm**
Replacement wire .... **No. 9 (Horolovar™ 0.004"/0.102mm)**
Replacement unit.......... **JS-S (Horolovar™ 6789)**
Jig settings................... **108mm, 114mm**
Mainspring .... **19 x 0.45 x 36mm (1140mm)**
Beats per minute........... **8**
Bob weight .... **370g.**

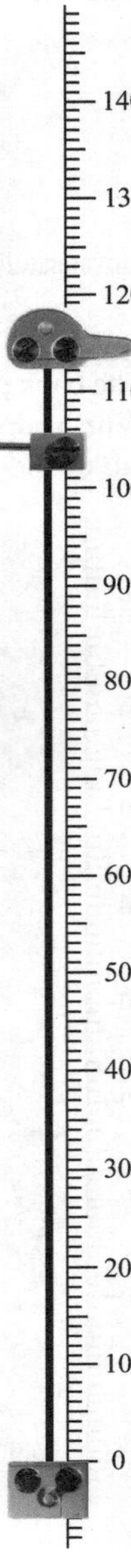

Examples of clocks fitted with the Würth Standard movement

INDEX

Rectangular

Reiner See Uhrenfabrik Herr/Reiner

Round

Schatz See Jahresuhrenfabrik Aug. Schatz

Schlenker & Posner

Schnekenburger

Shmid-Schlenker W. A.

Siegfried Haller

Other Anniversary Clock books by the author

ANNIVERSARY CLOCK ADJUSTING

by Mervyn Passmore

Anyone can set up and adjust these delicate 400 day or Anniversary clocks, but succeeding in doing so quickly and properly only comes with a knowledge of how they work and the correct sequence to do things in.

Mervyn Passmore explains in simple layman's language what to do, how to do it and when. In 1976 he co-founded one of the world's leading distributors of clockmakers' supplies and the vast experience he has acquired in supervising technical support to their customers has been put to good use here.

Translations into French & German

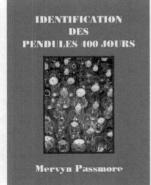